HEROES OF HISTORY

WINSTON CHURCHILL

Resolute

JANET & GEOFF BENGE

Emerald Books

P.O. BOX 635, LYNNWOOD, WA 98046

Emerald Books are distributed through YWAM Publishing. For a full list of titles, including other great biographies, visit our website at www.emeraldbooks.com.

Winston Churchill: Resolute

Published by Emerald Books
P.O. Box 635
Lynnwood, WA 98046

Cataloging-in-Publication Data is on file at the Library of Congress.

ISBN 978-1-62486-153-6

First printing 2023

Printed in the United States of America

HEROES OF HISTORY

WINSTON CHURCHILL

Resolute

HEROES OF HISTORY

Abraham Lincoln
Alan Shepard
Ben Carson
Benjamin Franklin
Benjamin Rush
Billy Graham
Captain John Smith
Christopher Columbus
Clara Barton
Davy Crockett
Daniel Boone
Douglas MacArthur
Dwight Eisenhower
Elizabeth Fry
Ernest Shackleton
Frederick Douglass
George Washington
George Washington Carver
Harriet Tubman
John Adams
Laura Ingalls Wilder
Louis Zamperini
Meriwether Lewis
Milton Hershey
Orville Wright
Ronald Reagan
Theodore Roosevelt
Thomas Edison
William Bradford
William Penn
William Wilberforce
Winston Churhill

Available in paperback, e-book, and audiobook formats.
Curriculum Guides are available for all of the U.S. biographies.
www.Heroesofhistory.com

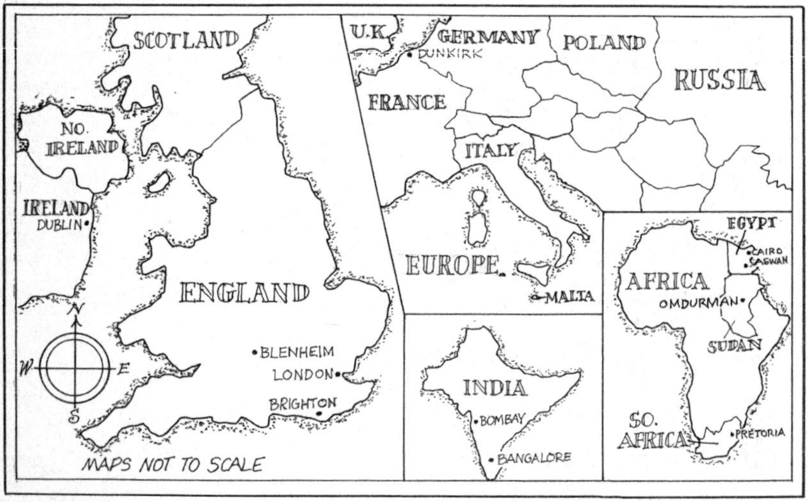
SCOTLAND
NO. IRELAND
IRELAND
DUBLIN
ENGLAND
BLENHEIM
LONDON
BRIGHTON
N
S
W
E
MAPS NOT TO SCALE
U.K.
GERMANY
DUNKIRK
POLAND
RUSSIA
FRANCE
ITALY
EUROPE
MALTA
INDIA
BOMBAY
BANGALORE
EGYPT
CAIRO
ASWAN
AFRICA
OMDURMAN
SUDAN
SO. AFRICA
PRETORIA

Contents

Chapter 1

Destiny Was At His Side

Winston Churchill leaned forward in his saddle. He gripped the reins firmly, so his horse didn't bolt until the bugle sounded. As he did so, he surveyed the enemy line before him. It consisted of several hundred Mahdists—Sudanese tribal fighters dressed in black and white robes. They stood defiantly about a hundred yards away, the curved blades of their razor-sharp swords glinting in the early morning African sun. In just a few seconds Winston and 310 other men of the 21st Lancers would be engulfed in a chaotic cavalry charge against them. It was a daunting moment, but one as an officer in Her Majesty's Army Winston was proud to be part of. The Lancers task this morning was to clear a path through the Sudanese fighters so an infantry column from Major General Kitchener's army could march through and capture the city of Omdurman.

When the bugle blast split the air, Winston dug his heels into his horse's flanks. The animal's nostrils flared as it surged forward in unison with the other Lancers. A rhythmic thud of hooves beating against the ground filled the air. As they approached, the Mahdists let out piercing cries and raised their swords ready for battle.

The crack of rifle-fire erupted from the Lancers, along with the clanging of swords. The men yelled and cursed at their enemy as fierce fighting erupted between the two sides. All the while the British cavalrymen moved their horses forward through the mayhem as fast as they could.

It didn't take long for the charging Lancers to break through the Mahdist line. Winston looked back at the swath they'd cut through the enemy. Many of them lay dead or wounded on the bloody ground. When he looked forward again, he realized they had only breached the first enemy line. When the Lancers began their charge, hidden from their line of sight in a fold of the ground were at least three thousand more Mahdist fighters, standing fourteen deep in some places. They surged forward. The odds of dying in the next minute suddenly increased. But there was no turning back now. This was not the time to give in to fear or doubt. They had a job to do, and Winston would do it or die trying. He urged his horse forward and the Lancers crashed into the second line of fighters.

Winston raised his pistol and shot at the first man he came to, and kept shooting as the enemy slashed at him with their swords. Finally, he made it through their line and reeled his horse to prepare for another charge. But the Mahdist fighters were fleeing before them; the battle was over. Winston and the other men of the 21st Lancers had cleared a path as ordered.

The Lancers next duty was to get their wounded comrades to the field hospital, all forty-nine of them. Following this, Winston helped collect the bodies of the twenty-one Lancers who had been killed in the fight. Their deaths needed to be documented and their bodies buried as quickly as possible.

Meanwhile, Major General Kitchener's infantry marched into Omdurman and subdued it. Now they were making their way over the Nile towards Khartoum, Sudan's capital, to capture it.

As he ate his field rations that night, Winston Churchill thought back to the moment he first saw the extra and unexpected three thousand Mahdist fighters before him. He fought hard against them and survived while nearly a quarter of his fellow Lancers either lay in shallow graves or on hospital cots. Goosebumps rose on his forearms. This was the third time in his twenty-three years of life Winston had faced stiff odds on the battlefield. Each of those times he came through the fight without a scratch. He had a strange feeling destiny was at his side, that he was being preserved for some higher calling; he just didn't know what it was…

Chapter 2

Phoenix Park

The day Mrs. Everest, his nanny, buttoned him into his new sailor suit, Winston Churchill understood that his grandfather was an important man. "Be a good boy," she told him, "and keep your hands inside the carriage. Everyone will be looking at you. Make your mother and father proud." Three-year-old Winston stood a little straighter.

Soon Winston was sitting beside his parents in the carriage in a parade of horses, soldiers, and dignitaries. Winston's grandfather, the duke of Marlborough and viceregent of Ireland, outranked them all. He was Queen Victoria's top representative in Ireland and lived at Phoenix Park, a large official estate in Dublin. Winston and his parents also lived at Phoenix Park in "The Little Lodge."

When the carriage came to a standstill, Winston took in the scene. A crowd was gathered in front of a huge object on a pedestal draped in a brown curtain. On either side of it were soldiers mounted on horseback. They wore scarlet dress uniforms with tall white plumes on their helmets. In front of them was row after row of foot soldiers in blue. A military band played "Rule Britannia." When the last notes of the tune faded, Winston watched his grandfather step onto a platform. Everyone clapped. As he listened to his grandfather speak, Winston tried to understand what the man was saying. When Winston's grandfather had finished his speech, he stepped over to the curtain and pulled a chord. The crowd cheered as the curtain opened to reveal a bronze statue of a military man on horseback. Winston thought he looked magnificent.

Later that evening, when his parents were attending an official reception, Winston asked his nanny about the statue. He trusted Mrs. Everest to help him understand certain things. He felt closer to her than anyone else on earth, mainly because his parents were away so often. Mrs. Everest told him that the man on horseback depicted in the statue was Lord Hugh Gough, who had won great battles in China and India that expanded the mighty British Empire. This made sense to Winston—war and empire were already familiar words to him and his grandfather and father often spoke of such things.

Winston understood that his father served as his grandfather's private secretary. Part of his duties, along with Winston's mother, Jennie, involved a lot of social engagements. Throughout the year they participated in various sporting events, including horse racing, steeple chasing, and fox and hare hunting. Winston's parents were avid horse people. His mother's father, Leonard Jerome, an American who lived in New York City, bred thoroughbred racehorses and had built the Jerome Park Racetrack. One house guest told Winston that his mother was the most fearless woman rider in Ireland. Winston believed him. When he was allowed to accompany her to the stables, he could see that she was never afraid of even the biggest stallion.

From his earliest memory, Winston tried to follow the conversations of the adults around him. His nanny gossiped about how dangerous Irish Catholics were, while his mother gushed over who would be attending the next fox hunt. And his father and grandfather were always talking about politics. This was because Winston's grandfather was a member of the House of Lords, the upper chamber of the British Parliament, while his father, Randolph, was a member of the House of Commons, the lower house of Parliament. Although they all lived in Ireland, Randolph continued to represent Woodstock and its surrounding area in Oxfordshire in England in the House of Commons. The Churchill family members were firm Conservatives, or Tories, as they called themselves. This meant they supported the High Church of England, Queen Victoria, and the right of the British Empire to rule its subjects with an iron hand. The Tories were led by Benjamin Disraeli, the current British prime minister. To fulfill their political obligations, Winston's grandfather and father made trips across the Irish Sea to London when Parliament was in session.

In early winter 1879, Winston's father returned from one of these trips with a trunkful of clothes. To Winston's surprise, the clothes were tiny, lacy gowns and tunics, which Mrs. Everest folded and placed in a nursery cupboard. Winston wondered who they were for. They certainly wouldn't fit him. The nanny explained to Winston that he would soon have a baby brother or sister. Winston wasn't impressed. He liked being an only child. He had observed other people's babies and thought they were no fun at all. A baby would not want to play trains with him and his new windup steam train or move toy cannons in a game of war.

On February 4, 1880, Mrs. Everest ushered five-year-old Winston into his mother's bedroom to meet his newborn brother. The baby's name was John Strange Spencer Churchill, but from the beginning everyone called him Jack.

At first Winston was scared. His new brother was born with blueish skin, and a church minister was called to baptize him without delay. Winston heard whispers that Jack might die. But Jack survived, and Mrs. Everest spent hours rocking him gently in Winston's old rocking chair. Winston felt jealous over this, but he could do nothing about it. Jack appeared to be here to stay.

Within weeks of Jack's birth, Winston learned that his life was in for another upheaval. There was an upcoming general election in England, and

Winston's parents needed to be there to campaign for his father's reelection. His grandfather's term as viceregent was ending at the same time.

The Churchill family's time in Ireland came to a close. Maids packed crates of dinnerware and trunks of clothes while Winston's mother prepared her favorite hunting horses for transport over the Irish Sea and his father supervised the packing of his books. In the nursery, Winston was allowed to pick twenty toy soldiers to take with him in his knapsack. He then watched as his nanny wrapped the rest in newspaper and packed them into an old hatbox for the journey back to England.

After the whirlwind of packing and saying goodbye, Randolph and Jennie Churchill, along with Winston and baby Jack, took the ferry to England and then a train to Woodstock where they rented hotel rooms in town. Winston's father began a vigorous campaign to keep his seat in Parliament. Once again, the election pitted William Gladstone and the Liberal Party against current prime minister, Benjamin Disraeli. Over the previous fifteen years, these two party leaders had taken turns winning elections and serving as either prime minister or leader of the opposition. In the April 1880 general election, Benjamin Disraeli and the Tories lost to William Gladstone and the Liberals, though Winston's father managed to win and retain his seat in the House of Commons representing Woodstock.

Once the election was over, the Churchill family had some time to relax. Winston often went with his father to visit his grandparents now living in

Blenheim Palace. Winston was amazed to think he had been born there. The palace was more magnificent than anything Winston had seen before, even grander than the viceregal's residence in Ireland. Six tall white columns flanked the front doors that opened into one of the palace's eight hundred rooms. Inside, everything Winston looked at had a family story behind it. Five tapestries made from wool and silk stretched from wall to wall and floor to ceiling. The tapestries depicted heroic scenes from the life of Winston's ancestor, John Churchill, First Duke of Marlborough. Winston loved to stare at the First Duke wearing a red coat with gold cuffs and a three-cornered hat and sitting astride a powerful white horse. Winston knew that Queen Anne and her Parliament had given John Churchill the land and money to build Blenheim Palace, along with a dukedom as reward for his military triumphs. He had led the British army against the French and Bavarians in the War of the Spanish Succession that culminated in the Battle of Blenheim in 1704.

Blenheim Palace felt like a museum dedicated to John Churchill and his wife, Sarah, who were both buried in a marble vault in the palace chapel. Many other dukes of Marlborough and their wives were buried under the chapel floor. Winston knew that his mother didn't like visiting the cold and drafty palace. She complained that there was nothing to do there, but Winston loved the pomp and ceremony of it all. He also liked spending time with four of his cousins, who stayed there for long stretches of time.

The cousins were the children of his father's older brother, Uncle George, and his wife, Aunt Goosie. Sunny was Winston's favorite cousin. He was three years older than Winston and the oldest son. This meant that he would eventually inherit the title of duke of Marlborough, along with Blenheim Palace and its two thousand acres of manicured grounds. On the other hand, Winston, as the son of a younger Churchill, would inherit almost nothing. Unlike Sunny, he would need a real job when he grew up.

Soon after the April election, Winston's family moved into 29 St. James Place, Mayfair, London. The brown brick building was four stories tall and shared side walls with neighboring houses. With a new home, life fit into a new routine. A tutor arrived to help Winston learn. Winston soon discovered he hated arithmetic. It infuriated him that he could get so close to the right answer, sometimes just one number away, and his tutor would mark it wrong. Shouldn't he get *some* credit for an answer that was *almost* right?

While he hated being tutored, Winston had a vague understanding that something worse awaited once he was too old for a tutor—boarding school. Cousin Sunny went to boarding school, as did his neighbor Harry. Every boy from an aristocratic family appeared to go to boarding school. This meant spending up to fifteen weeks at a time away from home and living in a dormitory with ten to twenty other boys. He had been told they did everything together—eat, study, and play cricket and rugby. Winston tried to convince himself it would be fun.

He imagined himself creeping out of the dormitory at night to raid the kitchen or paying one of the other boys to solve his arithmetic problems. He even pictured himself setting up elaborate war games on a sports field. Deep inside, however, Winston was anxious about boarding school.

One day Winston told his nanny he was looking forward to celebrating his eighth birthday on November 30 with her and his brother, Jack. Mrs. Everest gently informed him they wouldn't be able to do that because he would be away at boarding school by then. Winston was stunned. Sure enough, on Friday, November 3, 1882, about four weeks before his birthday, Winston's mother dropped him off at St. George's School near Ascot, thirty-five miles away from his home in London. As far as Winston was concerned, it may as well have been thirty-five hundred miles away.

Chapter 3

He Cannot Be Trusted To Behave Himself Anywhere

The clock on the wall at St. George's School chimed half past three. A tall schoolmaster in a black gown swept into the classroom. "Ah, Churchill," he said, "let's see what you're made of." He picked up a slim green book from a pile and opened it. "You haven't studied Latin yet, have you?"

"No sir," Winston replied.

"This book has the rudiments of Latin grammar," the master said, flicking through the pages at the front. "Yes, this will do. Learn these declensions of "mensa." I'll be back in a half hour to test you."

Winston stared at the open page of the book the teacher handed him. On one side of it were listed six words, one under the other: Mensa, Mensa, Mensam,

Mensae, Mensae, and Mensa. On the other side of the page opposite each word was a matching phrase, a table; O table; a table; of a table; to or for a table; and by, with, or from a table. What did this mean? Winston had no idea. As he stared at the list, he could see three of the words were spelled mensa, two mensae, and one mensam. Two of the corresponding phrases were "a table" and four other phrases involving tables that were different from each other.

Rubbing his forehead, Winston went to work. While he didn't understand anything about grammar, he did know how to memorize. One of his favorite pastimes was memorizing poems. Although he didn't have many boys to compare himself to, his mother told him he had an exceptionally good memory. By the time the schoolmaster reentered the room, Winston had the two lists perfectly memorized.

"Did you learn the declensions for mensa?" the master asked.

Winston nodded hesitantly. "I can say them, sir."

The master nodded. "Go on then. I don't have all day."

Winston began recounting the list, "Mensa—a table. Mensa—O table. Mensam…," and on he went.

"Well done," the schoolmaster said when Winston had finished.

Winston allowed himself a smile. He'd passed his first test. But he wanted to know more about Latin. "But what does it all mean?" he asked.

"Mensa is Latin for table, of course, followed by declensions in order: the nominative, vocative, accusative, genitive, dative, ablative."

"Oh," Winston replied. He had no idea what the teacher was talking about.

"But what does 'O table' mean?" he gingerly inquired.

The schoolmaster's eyes bored into Winston. "O table is the vocative case. One would use it to address a table."

Astonished, Winston blurted, "But I would never speak to a table!"

The master's eyebrows raised abruptly. "If you continue down this road of impertinence, young man, you'll be punished until you come into line. And your punishment will hurt. I can assure you of that."

Winston fell silent. Within an hour of arriving at St. George's School he'd gotten off on the wrong foot, as his nanny would have described it, and he didn't know how to make things better. He already knew he hated Latin. If he'd uncovered something as silly as how to address a table in his first lesson, how many other useless declensions would he be forced to learn? And what exactly was the punishment he would receive if he didn't concentrate on his work?

That night Winston lay in bed in the room he shared with six other boys, trying to cheer himself up. On the good side he was surprised the school was fitted with electric lights. Electric lighting was very new, and few places had it. Because of Winston's father's connection to a fledgling electric company, the Churchill home in London was about to become the first house in the city to have electric lights installed. On the bad side, the boys at the school seemed cliquish, but perhaps that was to be expected as they were seven weeks into their autumn term when Winston arrived.

Winston hoped he could make friends over time. But the lessons—that was another matter. His mother told him she had chosen St. George's School partly because there were only ten boys in each class, and Winston would get plenty of individual attention from the various teachers. Winston, though, saw the small class size as something to dread. There would be no hiding in the middle of the pack. The eyes of his teachers would be constantly on him. Already Winston knew he was going to struggle at Latin. He liked things to make sense, and up until now, someone, usually Mrs. Everest had the time to answer his every question. But in St. George's School, it seemed asking questions was dangerous. Winston always had questions. He wanted to know things. As he suspected the first night, this proved to be a terrible trait for an eight-year-old boy under the authority of a headmaster like the Reverend Herbert W. Sneyd-Kynnersley.

No matter what Winston did or how hard he tried, things seemed to get worse. St. George's School was ruled with fear—fear of getting a bad grade, fear of being told on by another boy, fear of being accused of not trying hard enough, fear of letting the team down while playing sports. There were more things that could go wrong for a student at the school than Winston could imagine. And whatever the infraction, the students were all punished in the same way: a flogging from the Reverend Sneyd-Kynnersley.

Before long, Winston learned of a ritual that horrified him. The students were all summoned to the library, where the names of boys needing "correction" were called. One by one, each of the boys marched into an adjoining room. Then, like clockwork, came the sound of a swish, a thwack, and a wail. "It's a birch stick," one of the other students whispered to Winston. "We do this once a fortnight." Winston winced. "Reverend Sneyd-Kynnersley strips us down and then just keeps striking us until he sees blood." Winston stood still trying to block out what he was hearing. He knew that no matter how hard he tried, he was sure to slip up. And this was what would be waiting for him.

Sure enough, a month later Winston's name was called. He trembled as he joined the line of boys awaiting their punishment. And it was every bit as brutal as Winston imagined it to be. Once inside the adjoining room, two senior boys told him to pull his pants down and then forced him to kneel for his beating. Being a redhead, Winston had sensitive skin, and he bled after only three stinging strokes from the birch.

Winston knew the punishment was meant to change his behavior, but it had the opposite effect. He all but dared the Reverend Sneyd-Kynnersley to flog him again. He felt no matter what he did or how hard he tried, it would never be good enough for the headmaster. So why try?

Although the boys were required to write letters home once a week, the letters were read by a proctor before being mailed. Winston didn't dare alert his parents or nanny as to what was happening at school. He lived for letters from home, many from Mrs. Everest, who described in detail brother Jack's goings on and the antics of the family cat. Occasionally Winston received a letter from his mother. Her letters were filled with news of her two sisters, Aunt Clara and Aunt Leonie, who, like his mother had both been born in New York City. They had all moved with his grandmother to Paris during the 1870s, while Winston's grandfather stayed behind in the United States. But the family members all visited each other regularly. Aunt Clara had married an Irishman named Moreton Frewen two years before and was now visiting London. The month before Winston started attending boarding school, Uncle Moreton had returned to their cattle ranching venture in Wyoming. His mother's description of life on the ranch sounded adventurous and Winston longed to visit the place himself. His mother also wrote to him about his father's constant travels, sometimes enclosing stamps from his letters. Winston would stare at them, hoping for some glimpse of the exotic life his father was leading while he was stuck in class at St. George's School.

In July 1883, after Winston had been attending the school for eight months, he was called to the headmaster's office, where he was informed that his grandfather, the seventh duke of Marlborough, had died of a heart attack. Winston's grandfather's death came as a surprise to everyone, as he was only sixty-one years old. Winston didn't attend his grandfather's funeral, but the next time he visited Blenheim Palace, things felt very different. His Uncle George was now the eighth duke of Marlborough and was in the process of divorcing Aunt Goosie. His grandmother had moved from the palace into a home in the fashionable Mayfair area of London. Winston's grandfather had left his grandmother in control of his money until she died. In the meantime, it cost thousands of pounds a year to pay for eighty staffers and the upkeep of Blenheim Palace. Winston's uncle constantly complained that he was running out of money for the upkeep of the palace.

Winston lived for the holidays, when he could return to Mrs. Everest, Jack, and his ever-growing collection of toy soldiers. During the Christmas holiday he counted them all—he had more than fifteen hundred toy soldiers. In the playroom, Winston and Jack would play with them for hours, lining them up on trestle tables in battle formation and executing intricate battle sequences.

Whenever Winston returned home from school, his stomach was always in a knot over his latest report card. If it was a particularly bad one, his father would read it aloud. "*Diligence:* Conduct has been exceedingly bad. He is not to be trusted to do any one thing. *Number of times late:* 20 times. Very disgraceful. Very bad. *General conduct:* Very bad. Is a constant trouble to everybody and is always in some scrape or other. *Headmaster's Remarks:* He cannot be trusted to behave himself anywhere." When the report card was bad, Winston's parents would make it clear to him how disappointed they were. Sometimes they yelled at him. At other times they bribed him to try harder. But nothing seemed to work.

When visiting home, Winston didn't dare tell anyone how miserable his life was at St. George's School. Nonetheless, it soon enough became known. Midway through the term, the Reverend Herbert Sneyd-Kynnersley sent Winston home to recover from a bout of asthma. The family physician, Dr. Roose, was called to the house in London to examine nine-year-old Winston. During his examination, the doctor was shocked to discover a crisscross of infections on Winston's upper thighs and buttocks. Winston explained they were the result of his numerous floggings at St. George's School. Winston's mother sprang into action. She promised him he would never have to see the Reverend Sneyd-Kynnersley again. Relief swept over Winston. It was worth having asthma just to hear such wonderful news.

Winston was enrolled in the Brighton School in Hove on the outskirts of Brighton on England's south coast. He would begin attending the school for the fall term in 1884. Dr. Roose highly recommended this school which was run by two sisters, Charlotte and Kate Thomson. His own son Bertie was a student there.

Dr. Roose was right. Brighton School was very different from St. George's. The Thomson sisters didn't believe in flogging and allowed the boys to choose some of their own activities. Winston chose extra swimming, horse riding, poetry, and history, along with collecting stamps and butterflies. It felt like heaven to him.

After completing their homework in the evenings, the boys were allowed to read. Winston had his favorite books: *Treasure Island, King Solomon's Mines,* G. A. Henty's *The Cornet of Horse: A Tale of Marlborough's Wars.* This last book was especially gripping because it was a fictional account of Rupert Holliday, a young man who went to battle in the War of the Spanish Succession under the command of Winston's ancestor, John Churchill, Lord Marlborough. Rupert survived imprisonment, escape attempts, duels, and all sorts of other adventures under the heroic leadership of Lord Marlborough. Winston marveled at the wonderful life his ancestor had lived and thought of the giant tapestries and other paintings of him hanging on the walls at Blenheim Palace depicting scenes that G. A. Henty had so vividly described in his book.

Miss Charlotte Thomson supplied newspapers for any boy who wished to learn about current events. These soon became Winston's favorite reading material. The front-page headlines were often about people in politics. Winston recognized many of their names. He'd even met some of them. Best of all, his father was featured in many articles. By now, Randolph Churchill was what his mother described as a rising star in the Conservative Party. Through reports in *The Times* and *The London Evening Standard,* Winston felt a real connection with his father and his political life. Better yet, Miss Thomson allowed him to keep the old newspapers. Winston meticulously cut out and pasted every article about his father into a large scrapbook. He loved to thumb through the collected reports. From them he also memorized entire speeches his father had given. He secretly recited them in front of the bathroom mirror while imagining that one day he would work beside his father.

In October 1884, Winston received a letter from his mother informing him that she and his father and Aunt Clara were off to New York City to attend the wedding of her sister and Winston's aunt, Leonie. Leonie was marrying John Leslie, the son of an Irish baron. No sooner had his parents returned from the wedding than Winston's father departed on a tour of India.

Winston followed his father's trip through reports in the newspapers. He plotted the places his father visited: Bombay, Lucknow, Calcutta, and Hyderabad. Winston's father was away for four months, and soon after his return to London, he was appointed Secretary of State for India. Winston was jubilant. He even wrote to his father asking for multiple copies of his autograph which he sold to his classmates.

In January 1886 newspapers in England carried more news about Randolph Churchill. As Secretary of State for India, he had ordered a surprise military invasion of Upper Burma. The territory was captured by British troops, and on New Year's Day, Upper Burma was officially declared a new province of India. It now belonged to the British Empire.

In the June 1886 British election, Randolph Churchill campaigned hard. In the election the Conservative Party won a sizeable parliamentary majority. The new prime minister, Lord Salisbury, rewarded his effort by making Randolf Chancellor of the Exchequer and Leader of the House of

Commons. This was the third most powerful political position in the government. Newspaper headlines predicted that Randolph was well on his way to becoming the prime minister of Great Britain. Eleven-year-old Winston was ecstatic. Of course, the newspaper predictions were right! Winston imagined himself returning from school to 10 Downing Street, the prime minister's official residence, and being allowed to sit in on all the political gossip shaping the country and empire. And his mother, who was still young and glamourous, would make a fine wife for a prime minister. Winston saw himself when he finished school becoming his father's private secretary, just has his father had been his grandfather's private secretary while he was viceregent of Ireland.

Four months later, Winston had a lot to follow in the newspapers. His father was embroiled in a public debate. As Chancellor of the Exchequer, his job was to propose the government's budget. He asked for many sweeping reforms, including cutting income taxes while raising taxes on luxury goods and tightening the budget of the army and navy. However, Lord Salisbury thought this was going too far. But Randolph Churchill decided to take a gamble, a gamble he was sure he would win. He wrote to Lord Salisbury tendering his resignation unless the budget proceeded through Parliament as written. He was confident that the Tories could not go on without him, their "rising star." He also gave *The Times* newspaper a copy of his letter, so that there could be no private reconciliation or backtracking. Much to Randolph's shock, Lord Salisbury accepted his resignation immediately. Randolph was out of a job. Winston read about all of this in the morning newspaper. He was old enough to understand that his father had taken a huge gamble and lost.

Overnight, all of Winston's dreams evaporated. There would be no 10 Downing Street, no late-night eavesdropping on important conversations. True, his father had not been removed from his seat in the House of Commons, but that was a long way from being prime-minister-in-waiting.

Christmas 1886 was grim for Winston and his brother Jack. Their father lay on the couch in the parlor under a cloud of cigarette smoke. Their mother slammed doors and stomped around in a terrible mood. Once Christmas was over, Randolph Churchill and a few close allies left on a trip to North Africa. Winston's mother told Winston that his father was sick and needed a complete rest. Winston wondered if he was really sick or just sick of politics.

For once Winston was glad to escape home and return to Brighton School for the spring term. There he played cricket and rugby and continued to swim and ride horses. In June his mother let him take time off school to attend Queen Victoria's Fiftieth Jubilee. Winston accompanied his mother to dinner aboard the royal yacht *Britannia* and met the Prince of Wales and his son George. Winston, though, was more impressed when the following day Uncle Moreton took him to meet his friend Buffalo Bill and watch his Wild West show.

In early 1888 Winston was in his last term at Brighton School. His parents had already decided where he would attend college. His father and his male ancestors all the way back to the mid 1700s had gone to Eton, but Dr. Roose warned about Winston's asthma. The ancient brick buildings of Eton College were built on the banks of the Thames near the heart of London. The combination of the river's dampness and the city's smog would be unhealthy. Dudley Marjoribanks, one of Winston's cousins, was being sent off to attend Harrow, a beautiful three hundred-acre estate set on a hill in the countryside northwest of London. It was decided that Winston and Dudley would attend Harrow together. Randolph and Jennie Churchill made it clear to their eldest son that they expected him to keep up with the smartest boys at Harrow. Winston didn't know how he was going to do that.

Chapter 4

So Regular in His Irregularity

It was a rainy morning in April 1888 when, for the third time in his life, Winston Churchill found himself walking through the gates of a new school. This time he was particularly nervous. The reputation of Harrow, the most expensive high school in England, dated back to 1572 when it was founded under a Royal Charter from Queen Elizabeth I. The school was steeped in tradition from its songs to its own set of rugby rules. Five British prime ministers had been educated there, along with countless politicians, intellectuals, and foreign royalty. As he climbed the school steps for the first time, Winston mused on all the things that could go wrong for him here.

Winston tried his best to settle into learning and school life. It wasn't easy. Many of his classmates had attended top prep schools and were far ahead of him in their studies. He was assigned to the bottom class of the lowest form, fourth form. As usual, he rose to the top in the subjects he loved and floundered in the others. Harrow had a high standard for conduct covering such things as arriving early or on time for class and wearing the correct components of the uniform to various school events and never arguing with school masters. Regrettably, Winston failed at each of these rules.

Three months after Winston first walked through the school's gate, Mr. Davidson, Winston's housemaster at Harrow, wrote to his parents.

> When a boy first comes to a public school, one always expects a certain amount of helplessness, owing to being left to himself so much more in regard to preparation of work etc. But a week or two is generally enough for a boy to get used to the ways of the place. Winston, I am sorry to say, has, if anything, gotten worse as the term passed. Constantly late for school, losing his books and papers, and various other things into which I need not enter—he is so regular in his irregularity that I really don't know what to do: and sometimes think he cannot help it...

As usual, Winston shrugged off the remarks in his housemaster's letter. As far as he was concerned, he was keeping quite busy at Harrow. He was an enthusiastic collector of bird's eggs and butterflies, and he still had his beloved stamp collection.

Winston also diligently applied himself to memorizing as many lines as possible from Thomas Macauley's book of poetry *Lays of Ancient Rome*. Harrow's English master offered a prize to the student who could remember the most lines of the poems. Thomas Macauley had served as a British official in India, and his work had taken him to numerous remote areas of the country. Wherever he was, whether trekking through the Neilgherry Hills of Southern India or sailing across the Bay of Bengal, he composed poems. Most were about the history of Rome, the wars it won, and the gallant men who fought in them. Winston particularly liked the first poem in the book. It was about Publius Horatius, who inspired two of his comrades to stay with him on the south side of the bridge over the Tiber River while the rest of the army demolished the bridge to cut Rome off from an attacking army. Horatius and his two companions expected to be killed holding the enemy at bay.

Then out spake brave Horatius,
The Captain of the Gate:
"To every man upon this earth
Death cometh soon or late.
And how can man die better
Than facing fearful odds,
For the ashes of his fathers,
And the temples of his gods...

"Haul down the bridge, Sir Consul,
With all the speed ye may;

I, with two more to help me,
Will hold the foe in play.
In yon strait path a thousand
May well be stopped by three.
Now who will stand on either hand,
And keep the bridge with me?"

Winston was inspired by Horatius's courageous actions. He loved the rhythm of the poem and spent hours in front of a mirror, memorizing the lines and acting them out at the same time. His hard work paid off. Winston was able to repeat twelve hundred lines from *Lays of Ancient Rome* without making a single error. It was enough lines to win the school prize, but not enough to stop his parents and school masters from nagging him to try harder.

Randolph and Jennie Churchill were home for Christmas, and Winston spent the holiday with them. Although now fourteen years old, Winston looked forward to playing war games with Jack. He spent many hours running over new maneuvers for his toy soldiers.

One afternoon, Winston's father came up to the nursery and stood watching his sons play. After a few minutes Winston noticed his father staring thoughtfully at him. "You seem to have an abiding interest in your soldiers. Would you like to go into the military?" he asked.

"Yes, I would," Winston replied, delighted that his father had recognized some potential in him.

After Christmas, Winston returned to Harrow, where he continued to try hard at the things he liked and ignore those things he didn't. He was constantly in trouble for breaking the rules. He got caned by one of the school masters for smashing windows in an empty factory nearby. He also took up smoking cigars, which, although not against school rules, was something his mother forbade. Winston promised her he would stop for six months, but at the end of that time he took it up again.

On March 3, 1891, during Winston's third year at Harrow, his mother sent a note informing him that his grandfather, Leonard Jerome, had died at Brighton. Leonard had been sick for several months and had sailed from New York City to be nursed by his wife and his daughters. Winston wished he'd known his grandfather Jerome Leonard better. Jerome was an accomplished horseman who had helped found the American Jockey Club. Winston was impressed when he read in the newspaper that Robert Todd Lincoln, Abraham Lincoln's son, attended his grandfather's funeral in his capacity as the United States Minister in the United Kingdom.

Soon after Winston's grandfather's death, Randolph Churchill set off on another trip, this time to South Africa. He had a contract with *The Daily Graphic* newspaper in London to write a series of articles about what he saw and any adventures he had along the way. Before he departed, Winston's father gave his son permission to transfer to the military track at Harrow. In this new track, Winston discovered that he was an excellent fencer, and his head was soon filled with thoughts of military grandeur. He'd read many novels based on war stories and heard countless tales about his ancestor the first duke of Marlborough, and he began to imagine his own future. Sometimes he had glimpses of astonishing possibilities that he felt were too preposterous to talk about. He worried people would laugh at his audacity.

One Sunday evening, Winston asked his school friend Murland Evans what he was considering doing when he left Harrow. Murland shrugged his shoulders and explained he had two options. Since he was doing so well in languages, he could join the Diplomatic Service, or he could follow his father into the field of finance. "Will you go into the army, or are you leaning towards politics, like your father?" Murland asked Winston.

"I don't know. I might," Winston replied. "I'm not afraid of public speaking. Most people are, you know. So that makes politics easier for me than for others."

"You don't seem at all clear about your intentions or desires," Murland noted with a frown.

Winston thought for a moment and pondered how truthful he should be. Did he trust Murland enough to tell him about his strange premonition? He decided to risk it. "The immediate future might still be shrouded, but I have a clear idea of where I will end up. I have dreams about it." Winston then went on to explain how he saw changes descending upon a now peaceful world. There would be great upheavals, terrible struggles, and wars people couldn't imagine. London would be in great danger. It would be attacked, and he, Winston Churchill, would play a prominent part in defending London.

Murland looked at him in disbelief. "How can you talk like that? England will never be invaded again. We haven't been under attack since the days of Napoleon!"

"I see farther ahead than you do," Winston responded. "I see into the future. This country will be somehow subjected to a tremendous invasion, by what means I do not know, but I tell you I shall be in command of the defense of London, and I shall save it and England from disaster."

"So, you'll be a general then, in command of the troops?"

Winston told Murland that he wasn't certain, that his dreams about the future were blurred. Yet one thing remained clear: London would be in danger, and given the high position he would hold, it would fall to him to save the British capital and its empire. When the conversation was over, Winston was grateful that Murland had taken him seriously, even if his dream sounded far-fetched.

In September 1892, Jack joined Winston at Harrow, and the two shared a room. Most people found it hard to believe the boys were brothers. Jack, with black hair and dark brown eyes, took after their mother, while Winston was the lone redhead in the family and had pale blue eyes. Their temperaments were even more different than their looks. Jack had come to Harrow at the top of his prep school. In fact, he'd done so well he was allowed to enter Harrow a year early. Studying math and languages came easily to him, subjects that Winston found nearly impossible.

During what Winston hoped would be his last term at Harrow and Jack's first, the brothers received news of another death in the family. This time it was Uncle George. At forty-eight years of age, George had dropped dead alone in his workshop at Blenheim Palace. Winston's thoughts went immediately to his twenty-year-old cousin Sunny, who now became the duke of Marlborough and a member of the House of Lords. If Sunny died before he had children of his own, Winston's father would inherit the title, and Winston would be next in line to be the duke.

Uncle George's death occurred three weeks before Winston's eighteenth birthday. Winston was busy studying for the entrance exam for the Royal Military Academy Sandhurst, where all British army officers were trained. Because Winston was distracted by all the family comings and goings around his uncle's funeral, he failed the entrance exam. Sandhurst took the top ninety students, and Winston came in 390th. He promised himself he would try harder and re-sit the exam in early January. If he didn't get into Sandhurst, he had no idea what he would do.

Winston sat the entrance exam again and then went on holiday with Jack, their mother, and their grandmother Churchill. They were all guests at Canford Manor, the home of Winston's aunt, Lady Wimborne. Winston always enjoyed visiting Canford Manor because three of his male cousins—Ivor, Christian, and Fred—were all around his age and had great fun building forts and playing war games together.

During one of their war games, Winston found himself trapped on a swing bridge, his brother blocking one end and his cousins the other. Not ready to surrender, he leapt off the bridge hoping to grasp the top branches of a nearby pine tree. But Winston misjudged the distance to the branches, missing them completely and falling thirty feet to the ground. Three days later Winston regained consciousness. He learned that he had ruptured one of his kidneys and injured his right shoulder. The doctor was unsure whether he would make a full recovery. Winston had plenty of time to lie in bed and wonder if his foolhardy act had cost him any chance at a military career.

Three weeks after his fall, Winston learned that he'd failed the Sandhurst entrance exam for a second time. By now he was recovering well, so his father enrolled him in Captain James's Cramming School. This sounded like hell to Winston, but he was desperate to get into Sandhurst and agreed to put himself through the torture. Winston's parents made clear to him that this was his last chance. If he didn't pass the exam this time, he was on his own.

By April 1893, Captain James had the same complaints about Winston as all his previous teachers. He wrote to Winston's father saying, "All the tutors complain that while he has good abilities, he does not apply himself with sufficient earnestness to his reading. He can and will succeed if he will but give up everything to the examination before him, but I doubt his passing if he will not do this."

In August, Winston sat the Sandhurst entry exam one last time. To his immense relief he passed, just barely, and was assigned to the cavalry, since he hadn't scored high enough to get into the more prestigious infantry. This did not impress his father, who complained that cavalrymen had to pay to transport and stable their own horse at a cost of two hundred pounds a year. Randolph Churchill wrote to Winston, warning him that he had better work hard at Sandhurst lest he become a useless human being and a drain on the family.

Chapter 5

He Needed a War!

It was Friday, September 1, 1893. Winston sat staring at the syllabus on the desk in front of him. *How marvelous*, he thought. Three terms of work—junior, intermediate, and senior—and not a single class in French, Greek, or Latin. That was all behind him now. For the next year he would study tactical maneuvers, bunker building, blowing up bridges, derailing trains, and constructing dugouts, along with how to maintain control of a horse at a parade and in combat. Gazing around the classroom, Winston realized for the first time in his education everyone was on a level playing field. None of his fellow cadets had studied these subjects before arriving at Sandhurst. No one came knowing how to design a zigzag trench. They would all learn together. For once Winston would have a chance to prove to his father he was as smart and capable as any of the other cadets.

At Sandhurst, Winston was finally able to deliver on his promise to work hard and earn good marks in his studies. He still made time to read about his father's exploits in the House of Commons. But he noticed the newspaper articles were getting shorter and more critical. They reported that Lord Randolph Churchill would often ramble off topic during his speeches and sometimes would even stop midsentence and sit down seemingly unaware of what he was doing.

This alarmed Winston, and when he returned home at weekends, he watched his father closely. He soon realized the newspaper reports were not exaggerating. If anything, they weren't reporting some of the man's oddest behavior. His father's moods would quickly swing, and he often muttered nonsensical ramblings. Not only that, but also he seemed physically weaker. He'd lost weight and breathed heavily after climbing the stairs. Winston wasn't surprised when his mother announced she was taking his father on a year-long round the world trip. She sold their house in London, cashed in some of Randolph's shares, and booked tickets for the trip. She also hired a doctor to accompany them, along with several maids and a valet.

Randolph and Jennie Churchill departed on their trip from Southampton in June 1894, when Winston was halfway through his training at Sandhurst. As he'd done so many times before, Winston tracked his parents' progress across the Atlantic Ocean to

New York City and then through Canada by rail to the West Coast of the United States. From there his parents traveled by ship to Japan, China, Burma, India, and Singapore. Winston saved the letters he received from them and added the foreign stamps to his collection.

Winston and his brother Jack were spending Christmas with their grandmother in her house at Grosvenor Square in London when their parents arrived back six months early. Winston had looked forward to finally receiving his father's praise for winning a place in the top ten cadets at Sandhurst, but with one look at his father, he knew it was too late to talk about such things. Randolph Churchill was weak and dazed. His mother, he was convinced, had brought him home to die.

Sure enough, early on the morning of January 24, 1895, as a blizzard howled and the Thames froze over, Winston was summoned to his father's bedside. He ran through the snow, praying that he would get there in time to say a final goodbye and hear a final word of validation, but he was too late. Lord Randolph Churchill's funeral was held in St. Martin's Church at Bladon, a short distance from Blenheim Palace. The church overflowed with those who had traveled from London and around Great Britain to pay their respects. Archibald Primrose, the British prime minister, gave the eulogy. Afterwards Winston, Jack, and their mother lingered by the gravesite watching the snow fall. Winston's thoughts were bitter. His father was just forty-five years old, and his grandfather and his Uncle George had also died young. Winston felt cheated of his father's presence and worried that he was destined to die young as well.

A month after his father's death, Winston was commissioned as a cavalry officer in the 4th Queen's Own Hussars. He was based at Aldershot Garrison, thirty miles south of London. For the first time that he could remember, he was not a student, and it felt glorious. Winston hired a batman who brought him breakfast in bed every morning and attended to his every need. When the nine o'clock bell rang, the barracks became a bustle of activity—two hours of riding practice, an hour with the horses in the stables, and an hour and a half of drills. Following lunch, Winston and the other members of the Hussars relaxed until dinner. Some played billiards, cards, and chess and, in Winston's case, endless chukkas of polo.

Sometimes Queen Victoria would arrive at the garrison in her carriage to watch the calvary, infantry, and artillery on parade. Winston loved the pomp and ceremony of hundreds of horses wheeling in unison and soldiers looking splendid in their scarlet and gold uniforms.

Now that he didn't have to take his father's expectations into account, Winston began to question what he wanted in life. He realized that while the military was a great launching point, he ultimately wanted to follow in his father's footsteps into politics. He was only twenty years old, too young to be elected in the House of Commons. In the meantime, he set his sights on making a name for himself in the military that would set him up for a future in politics. He wrote in his diary,

> It is a fine game to play—the game of politics—and it is well worth waiting for a good hand before really plunging. At any rate, four years of healthy and pleasant existence—combined with both responsibility and discipline—can do no harm to me, but rather good. The more I see of soldiering the more I like it, but the more I feel convinced that it is not my métier.

While at Aldershot, Winston didn't see his mother often. His grandmother, Clara Jerome, was ill in Kent, and his mother and aunts tended to her. It was a blow to everyone when she died just three months after Winston's father. Then another three months later, Winston received a letter from Mrs. Everest's sister, Emma, informing him his old nanny was seriously ill. He asked for emergency leave and headed to London to be with her. As he sat on the train he thought of everything his nanny had meant to him. She was the one who had taught him to talk and had listened to his childish stories. And when he needed comfort, she would sit him on her lap and hug him. No one in the world understood him like Mrs. Everest. Surely, Winston tried to reassure himself, he wasn't losing her, too.

Upon arrival in London, Winston quickly saw that the situation was grave. Emma explained that her sister had peritonitis and her only request was to see Winston one more time. Winston swung into action, summoning his father's doctor and hiring a nurse for Mrs. Everest. But nothing could be done. Winston held her hand as she drifted in and out of consciousness. He was grateful that she recognized him. Mrs. Everest died the following morning, and Winston wept as he sat at her bedside. Winston took it upon himself to arrange and pay for her funeral. He then hired a local woman to make sure that Mrs. Everest's grave was always neat and tidy. He knew that his nanny would have appreciated that.

With the death of Mrs. Everest, another link to Winston's childhood was gone. He wondered who might be the next to die. In the space of six months he'd lost his father, grandmother, and nanny. Winston longed for a change of scenery, something new to keep his mind busy. He needed a war!

Sadly for Winston, however, the British Empire was experiencing a lull in battles, although one was going on in Cuba. Many Cubans, led by Maximo Gomez, had revolted against their Spanish colonial overlords. Captain General of Spain, Marshall Martinez Campos, had recently been sent across the Atlantic Ocean to restore order on the Caribbean Island. From what Winston had learned, most of the fighting involved small skirmishes—not the kind of grand war his forebear the duke of Marlborough had waged, but a war nonetheless. Winston knew that as an officer in the British army he couldn't join the Spanish army but hoped to go to Cuba as an official British observer.

During the five months over winter, military establishments in England all took leave. Most of

Winston's friends were going fox hunting or following the horse racing circuit, but he set his sights on the war in Cuba. He asked a fellow officer, Reggie Barnes, to go with him. He then wrote to some of his father's old friends, including Lord Wolseley, the commander in chief of the British army. He asked them to provide letters of introduction for Winston and Reggie to the Spanish commander in Cuba.

Winston then had another idea. He remembered that his father had written newspaper articles during his visit to South Africa. He approached *The Daily Graphic* newspaper, asking the newspaper's publisher to commission him to write a series of letters or reports from the front in Cuba. The publisher agreed and offered Winston the sum of five guineas for each letter he sent them for publication. Winston was in business. He could further both his military and his political aspirations at the same time, as long as he didn't get himself killed.

Winston's mother encouraged him to go, especially since he might possibly arrive in New York City by November 6, in time to attend the wedding of his cousin Sunny, the duke of Marlborough. Sunny was traveling to New York to marry American heiress, Consuelo Vanderbilt, the great-granddaughter of American railroad tycoon Cornelius Vanderbilt. Even though neither of them wanted to marry the other, their families had put pressure on them to do so. Sunny would receive a dowry of $2.5 million in US dollars from Consuelo's father for marrying his daughter, enough to fix up Blenheim Palace, while Consuelo would appease her mother, who desperately wanted a link to British aristocracy. Winston's mother also arranged for him and Reggie to stay with a friend she'd met in Paris, William Bourke Cockran, a wealthy Irish American lawyer and United States congressman famous for his oratory skills.

Winston and Reggie sailed off on their adventure aboard the Royal Mail steamship *Etruria* on November 2, 1895. The small steamship plowed through pounding winter storms on its seven-day voyage across the Atlantic Ocean. The men arrived two days behind schedule, causing Winston to miss his cousin's wedding. Nonetheless, Bourke was quayside when they arrived in New York and whisked them away to his extravagant Fifth Avenue apartment. Winston and Reggie were honored at a diamond-studded dinner party that night and then taken by his mother's cousin, Eva Purdy, to see the town. Their carriage drove them by the Jerome mansion situated across from Madison Square Park. The mansion was now a private club, but Eva gushed about how it was when Winston's mother grew up there. The mansion housed a six-hundred-seat theater, a breakfast room that could serve seventy people, and a white and gold ballroom with champagne and cologne fountains. It wasn't as sprawling as Blenheim Palace but was grander than Winston expected it to be.

As a wealthy United States congressman, Bourke Cockran opened many doors for the two young military men from Great Britain. They toured the Military Academy at West Point, boarded a battleship in New York Harbor, attended the New York Horse

Show, watched a demonstration of the latest firefighting techniques staged for them, and even spent a day with front-row seats at an infamous murder trial.

Between their hectic rounds of engagements Bourke spent many hours discussing politics with Winston and advising him on how to get ahead. According to him it all came down to making engaging speeches. The formula for that was simple: speak the truth and make one simple bold point and keep pounding on it with many illustrations and interesting examples. Nothing more was required. It was an easy formula, one Winston thought he could master.

Winston and Reggie stayed with Bourke for nine days and then boarded a private car for the train ride to Tampa, Florida. Once there they boarded the steamer *Olivette* for a 350-mile sea voyage to Cuba. Winston was on the deck of the *Olivette* as Cuba came into view and Morro Castle appeared ahead against the dawn sky. This imposing clifftop fortress guarded the entrance to Havana's harbor.

After a thorough search by customs officers Winston and Reggie stepped ashore. They hailed a horse and cab to take them to the Gran Hotel de Inglaterra. From there they set out for the Spanish government headquarters to present their letters of introduction to the consul general. There they learned that most of the Spanish troops were situated 150 miles east of Havana at Santa Clara under the command of Marshall Martinez Campos. That, according to the consul general, would be the best place for them to start.

On the way back to their hotel, Winston stopped at a factory shop to buy a box of hand-rolled Romeo y Julieta cigars. He'd already developed a taste for cigars and knew that Cuban cigars were of the highest quality. Surely, he reasoned, with action only days away, it was time to enjoy some rum and a good cigar to celebrate.

The following day Winston and Reggie were up early for the twelve-hour train ride east through the towns of Matanzas and Colon and on to Santa Clara. About halfway through the trip, their train was shunted onto a siding. Word reached Winston and Reggie that the railway track ahead had been cut, derailing an earlier train and seriously injuring fifteen passengers. The delay lasted for three hours while the track was repaired.

When their train reached its destination, Winston learned that General Juarez Valdez and three thousand men had recently left Santa Clara. They were marching forty miles southeast through the jungle to Sancti Spiritus. A military officer issued the two men guns for self-defense and provided them the paperwork necessary to travel by train and steamer to Santi Spiritus. With any luck, the officer explained, Winston and Reggie should arrive a day before the soldiers, whom they could then accompany and observe.

That night Winston wrote his first report. He included a sketch of a Spanish post near Santa Clara and described the advantages the Cuban rebels appeared to have over the Spanish troops. The rebels had the support of local people which meant they could move around the island blending in with them, even stopping to do manual labor to complete their disguise if necessary. They didn't wear uniforms, but they carried badges to identify themselves, nor did they adhere to any standard European conventions of war. Winston found it interesting and wrote that he could understand why Americans and others sympathized with the rebels and their plight on the island.

The next day Winston and Reggie caught the train to Cienfuegos, where they transferred to a steamer that transported them down Cuba's coast to Tunas. Then it was another train journey north to Sancti Spiritus. Winston and Reggie arrived first. They were welcomed and taken care of at Sancti Spiritus. The following morning the three thousand Spanish troops marched into town. Winston was surprised at how fit they all looked. He doubted that British troops would look so good after slogging for miles through tropical jungle.

Winston and Reggie introduced themselves to General Juarez Valdez and learned that he planned to continue their march at daybreak the following morning. The general explained that their mission was to kill as many rebels as possible as well as to check the villages and towns in the surrounding area that were under the protection of Spanish troops. The general himself was going to lead six hundred infantry and three hundred calvary soldiers northeast towards Arroyo Blanco. A heliographic station was located there, and he wanted to check on it. He invited Winston and Reggie to join them.

That night, Winston was so excited he could barely sleep. He was off to participate in a real war!

At 7 a.m. the following morning, he mounted a horse General Valdez had provided and they were off. The infantry moved in a single column through the dense jungle, slashing vines as they went, using a machete, a tool Winston had never seen before. One of the officers explained that the long knifelike implement was designed for slashing sugarcane, and Spanish soldiers in Cuba had been issued them. Not only was a machete useful in hacking through jungle undergrowth and vines, but also it was a deadly and efficient weapon. It could lop off a man's head with one blow.

After their evening meal, Winston wrote a draft of his second report from Cuba, noting that he was disappointed he hadn't glimpsed a rebel or seen any evidence of their being in the area. As the men marched on the next day and the day after that, from time to time they came across a hastily abandoned fire or were shot at through the dense jungle foliage.

On Friday afternoon, November 29, 1895, the soldiers under General Valdez's command reached Arroyo Blanco. It was time to check on the heliographic station perched on the summit of a nearby hill. A heliograph was a signaling device that could be used to transmit and receive Morse code messages using sunlight and mirrors. A message could be seen up to thirty-five miles away, all the way to Sancti Spiritus. Winston was fascinated to see this new communication apparatus in action.

Later that night, back at camp, General Valdez informed Winston that rebel leader Maximo Gomez and four thousand of his men were encamped just five miles east of their position. The general explained that at daybreak they would arise and attack the rebel camp. Winston prepared for his first real battle.

Winston was so excited the following morning that he almost forgot it was his twenty-first birthday. If he had been back in England, he would have spent the day being toasted with champagne and fox hunting. But out in the Cuban jungle he hoped the day would bring far more excitement than that. As Winston and Reggie accompanied the Spanish army they experienced a few skirmishes with the rebels but nothing spectacular enough for Winston. After a long day in the tropical heat, they made camp for the night.

The cooks quickly produced a meal of chicken and rice. As Winston sat eating it, a bullet whizzed past him. It hit a horse tethered a foot behind him. The horse collapsed, dead. Winston dived for cover as Spanish soldiers grabbed their rifles and returned fire. But as quickly as they struck, the rebel fighters melded back into the jungle. Winston had wanted action, and now he'd experienced it. Still, he was a little startled that he'd come within a foot of being shot in the head. It was something to think about.

The next day the column of soldiers moved on. As with the day before, there were many small skirmishes with rebel fighters who would suddenly appear from the undergrowth, fire their rifles, and just as quickly disappear back into the jungle. The next day though, the two sides came face to face in battle. The Spanish force was marching through a clearing when the Cuban rebels opened fire on them with volley after volley of bullets. The Spanish soldiers remained in formation and continued marching forward, firing as they went.

Five minutes later, it was all over, except for the smell of gunpowder in the air. The Cuban rebels retreated, and Winston looked around at the dead and wounded soldiers and rebel fighters. He wondered what the point of the battle had been. He didn't have time to dwell on it, however. By now it was time for Winston and Reggie to return to England via New York. General Valdez's troops needed to be reprovisioned as well. The general escorted Winston and Reggie back to Tunas, where they parted ways. The two young men retraced their journey back to Havana.

As he sailed out of Havana bound for Tampa, Florida, Winston tried to make sense of his experience in Cuba and the civil war that had engulfed the island. As a British cavalry officer, he understood the position that Spain, a European country with an empire, found itself in. He knew it was important for the Spanish to retain control of their Cuban colony and its resources. After all, he was sure the British would do the same if one of their colonies rebelled.

From Tampa Winston and Reggie returned to New York City, where they spent several more days with Bourke. On December 14, 1895, they boarded the *Etruria* once more for the trip back across the Atlantic Ocean. If all went well, Winston would be home in time for Christmas.

As the United States faded from view, Winston felt satisfied with his trip to Cuba. He had turned twenty-one years old there, had come under fire in battle for the first time, and had been able to write about it in reports for *The Daily Graphic*. Even so, he was unsettled. He thought back to his collection of over fifteen hundred lead toy soldiers and how he and his brother Jack used to line them up on trestle tables in battle formation, each commanding an army against the other. Now he had finally been in a real battle, and it wasn't nearly as glorious as he'd imagined it would be.

Chapter 6

Malakand Field Force

In January 1896, Winston learned that his regiment was being posted to India in September. This meant that he had nine months of light duties at the Aldershot Garrison before departure. This would give him plenty of spare time to indulge in regular upper-class pastimes, from masquerade parties to fox hunts and yachting regattas. It also gave Winston time to find a way to exchange his upcoming posting to India for something more exciting. The 4th Queen's Own Hussars were being assigned to India for a nine-year tour, and he hated to think of spending all that time performing garrison duty with little chance of real action. In August he wrote to his mother, begging her to pull some official strings on his behalf. "It is useless to preach the gospel of patience to me. Others as young [as me] are making the run now, and what chance have I of ever catching up?"

Despite his best efforts and his mother's many connections, Winston set sail with twelve hundred cavalry men for Bombay, India, aboard the SS *Britannia.* The ship steamed into the Atlantic Ocean, down the coast of Portugal, and into the Mediterranean Sea. As they approached the Suez Canal, Winston's spirits were low. He tried to distract himself from his fate by playing endless games of chess and listening to a string quartet that played in the evenings. But no matter what he did, he could feel his impatience rising. He simply could not be inactive in India for nine whole years.

Twenty-three days after setting out, the SS *Britannia* dropped anchor in Bombay Harbor. Lighter boats came alongside to ferry the men ashore, and Winston was one of the first on board. The rowers maneuvered the lighter boat alongside a quay, where slippery stone steps led up from the waterline. Winston reached up and grabbed a metal ring on the quayside as he steadied himself to transfer from the boat onto the steps. Suddenly, as he was about to step out, the boat dropped five feet in the swell. Winston felt a jolt of searing pain shoot through his shoulder as he clung to the ring. He let go and fell back into the boat. He tried again and felt his boots on the step. Although he didn't admit it to anyone, Winston was in excruciating pain. He knew he'd reinjured the same shoulder he had hurt three years before when he fell thirty feet from the swing bridge to the ground.

The regiment spent their first night in India camped out in double fly tents at the edge of Bombay. Winston barely slept because of the pain in his shoulder. At dawn the next morning the men climbed aboard a train headed for Bangalore, 620 miles south. Thirty-six bone-jarring hours later the train arrived at its destination. Winston already knew that Bangalore was one of the most coveted assignments in the British army. Now he could see why. The city reminded him of an English town. There was even a palace modeled after Windsor Castle in England.

Winston knew the history of the British in India from his history classes at Harrow. In 1600 the British East India Company began trading with some of the Indian states. Slowly the company's relationship had turned from simply being trading partners to bargaining with Indian rulers to take over their land and collect taxes from the local people. For 250 years the company played a complicated game keeping the 602 Indian states with their many religions, languages, allies, and enemies under its thumb. Then in 1857, Indians revolted against the British East India Company. After a series of bloody battles, the British government took over directly ruling India. Thus began the rule of the British Raj, whereby Queen Victoria appointed a viceroy to rule in her name over India's approximately 200 million new subjects. Now, forty years later, 240 million Indians were kept in check by the presence of approximately 73,000 British military officers and 157,000 Indian soldiers who served under them. Now Winston became one of those military officers.

Within a week of arriving, Winston had all the trappings of an up-and-coming subaltern in the British Armed Forces. Since Indian labor was cheap, he was able to hire three private servants: a dressing boy, a butler, and a groom. He, along with Reggie Barnes and another friend of theirs, was also able to rent a large pink-and-white bungalow. The men pooled their money and hired two men to take care of the two acres of beautiful gardens, along with three water carriers, four washerwomen, and a watchman.

Life in Bangalore fell into a leisurely routine. Each morning Winston arose at dawn for a mounted parade at 6 a.m. This was followed by an hour and a half of drills and maneuvers before he retired to take a bath and enjoy breakfast. By then it was 10 a.m., and he and his fellow officers rested until 5 p.m., when the cavalry officers met for polo matches. Winston didn't let his injury stop him from playing. He strapped his right arm to his chest and played left-handed. Following polo, it was time for another bath and then dinner at 8:30 p.m., at which time the regimental band serenaded them.

Winston methodically collected sixty-five species of exotic butterflies and grew fifty varieties of roses in the courtyard. It was a grand life for someone without ambition, but just as he'd predicted, Winston was soon bored. He looked around for other things that would interest him. To his surprise, he developed a curiosity for history and philosophy. He decided to use his spare time to undertake some serious study.

Winston wrote his mother a letter asking her to send some of his father's books. When they arrived,

Winston spent five hours each afternoon reading. He started with Edward Gibbon's *The History of the Decline and Fall of the Roman Empire* and Thomas Macaulay's twelve-volume *History of England.* When he wasn't reading, he was busy writing letters to his mother, Jack, Bourke in New York, and other friends and relatives. He also began writing a romantic novel set in a fictional country during a revolution.

But what Winston desperately wanted was a real war to write about. Ten months after his arrival in India, he heard reports of an uprising in Malakand, the farthest British outpost in northwest India. British troops had been dispatched to regain control in the area. Malakand consisted of three princely states: Chitral, Dir, and Swat. Princely states were not under direct British rule but had been coerced into being British allies. This was especially important in Malakand, which formed a buffer zone between British India and Afghanistan, which was under Russian influence. Winston knew he had to find a way to get there.

Winston began his quest in the usual way. He wrote to General Sir Bindon Blood, who had been chosen to lead twelve hundred British soldiers to be known as the Malakand Field Force. This force was tasked with infiltrating the river valleys of Malakand and neutralizing the Pashtun tribes that participated in the rebellion. Winston desperately wanted a temporary assignment to the new force. After a long delay, General Blood wrote back to say he didn't have authority over which soldiers joined the Malakand Field Force. However, if Winston was determined to join the fight, he would accept him as a war correspondent, providing he arrived with the right credentials.

Winston immediately wrote to his mother to enlist her help. In no time she had organized a deal for him with *The Daily Telegraph* in London to write a series of "Letters from the Front." The London newspaper would pay him five pounds for each letter. Winston also lobbied an Indian newspaper, *The Pioneer*, which contracted him to telegraph them three hundred words a day updating the latest news from Malakand.

With his press contracts in hand, Winston arrived at the train station in Bangalore on August 28, 1897. He stepped up to the ticket window to buy a ticket to Nowshera, the nearest railhead to where the Malakand Field Force was assembling. He was astonished to learn that Nowshera was 2,027 miles away. For the first time, Winston was beginning to comprehend just how immense India, the "Jewel of the British Empire," was.

The train trip from Southern India to its northern frontier took five days. Once Winston arrived at Nowshera, he still had fifty miles of desolate country to travel through. His only choice of transport was an ancient cart pulled by ponies that bumped along at seven miles an hour.

Exhausted, and with an aching shoulder, Winston arrived at the Malakand Field Force encampment. The location was rocky and hotter than anything Winston had ever experienced. That night, he wrote to his mother, urging her not to worry about him. He assured her that the risk he was taking would pay off in the end. He wrote, "I feel that the fact of having seen service with British troops while still a young man must give me more weight politically, must add to my claims to be listened to, and may perhaps improve my prospects of gaining popularity with the country. Besides this, I think I am of an adventurous disposition and shall enjoy myself not so much in spite of as because of the risks I run."

On Monday, September 6, 1897, Winston mounted his horse and rode out of camp with the rest of the Malakand Field Force. While most war correspondents stayed back from the action and wrote dispatches based upon what returning soldiers told them, Winston fully expected to be in the thick of battle. Clouds of dust billowed from the horses' hooves as they walked along a mountain track. The force then descended into the Lower Swat Valley and made their way to a rope suspension bridge spanning the River Swat. This was Chakdara, and a large stone fort loomed above the bridge to protect it. A bitter battle was fought for control of the fort and the bridge during the uprising.

Winston learned that the Pashtun tribes throughout the region knew how to use the dusty, rocky natural landscape to camouflage themselves, allowing them to attack from what seemed out of nowhere. This reminded him of the rebels in Cuba, who knew how to blend into their jungle surroundings but with one key difference. The rebels would open fire and then disappear back into the jungle as fast as they came. But according to the soldiers who'd engaged them during the uprising, the Pashtun tribesmen were fearless fighters who refused to retreat, preferring to fight to the death.

Late in the afternoon General Blood called for the force to encamp. Although Winston assumed they would pitch tents, the soldiers dug trenches to sleep in. When Winston joined them, he soon understood why. As the sun went down, bullets started whizzing over the trenches. Had the men been in their tents, they would have been sitting ducks.

At dawn the following morning they broke camp and rode deeper into the valley. Tribal snipers took shots at them, but the force kept moving. And that night Winston dug himself another sleeping trench. Once more, through the darkness the tribesmen strafed the camp with rifle fire. This went on for several more nights until on the morning of September 15, 1897, something occurred to break the pattern. An Indian officer galloped into camp at breakfast to report a brigade from the Malakand Field Force had been attacked during the night in the Mohmand Valley. Three British officers had been killed, along with twelve Indian soldiers. General Blood gave immediate orders for a contingent of soldiers to head into the Mohmand Valley and avenge the killing of the British and Indian soldiers. Winston asked to go with them.

The soldiers galloped through narrow canyons to the site where the brigade had been attacked and camped there for the night. Early the next morning they divided into three groups. Winston and the soldiers with him set off for the villages of Badelai and

Shahi-Tangi. Their mission was to obliterate them. As they got nearer, Pashtun tribesmen fired at them.

By eleven o'clock the men reached the village of Shahi-Tangi located on a hillside spur. They expected stiff resistance, but there was none. The village appeared to be deserted. The soldiers punched holes in the roofs of the mud huts with their rifle butts and threw flaming rags into them. One after the other, the huts burst into flames and smoke billowed. Suddenly, a band of tribesmen swooped down on them with a hail of gunshot. More men emerged, running and yelling, swords drawn. Winston was stunned by how fast and fearless they were. The scene quickly turned into a bloodbath. Swords glinted, the dusty rocks dripped crimson, horses collapsed, soldiers stumbled. Winston couldn't remain an observer, and he drew his pistol and fired. Moments later he heard the bugle sound retreat. Their hut burning had turned into a nightmare. Each soldier made his way down the hill any way he could, some propping up their wounded comrades. Several dead had to be left where they fell. Winston knew he would never forget the awful sight. As the soldiers reached the bottom of the spur, the artillery regrouped and opened fire on the tribesmen. It didn't take long for the British to gain the upper hand, and the tribesmen fled. The soldiers climbed back up the spur to claim their dead.

Over the next two weeks the Malakand Field Force made its way through the valleys of the area, destroying villages and disarming their inhabitants just like the action Winston had participated in. One by one the Pashtun tribes surrendered their weapons and submitted to the British.

In early October Winston received orders to return to the 4th Queen's Own Hussars in Bangalore. He'd been gone for nearly two months. His time as a roving war reporter was over. He had been in the thick of serious military action, and he felt pride in being a member of Her Majesty's army. But his pride was tinged with doubts. The battles he'd witnessed left a residue of distain for the brutality he witnessed.

Back in Bangalore, Winston set to work writing a book about the military excursion in the North West territories. Because he knew that the British public had a short attention span and that reports on the Malakand action would soon lose their appeal, he wrote during every spare minute he had. He hoped to have the book finished by Christmas. He was a week late, but on New Year's Eve he finished the last page of the 330-page manuscript. He titled it *The Story of the Malakand Field Force*, wrapped it in brown paper, and sent it off to the publisher in London.

Satisfied with his work, Winston puffed on a cigar and drank a glass of whiskey to celebrate. Tomorrow would be New Year's Day 1898. It was time to set his sights on the next war zone. Where would that be?

Chapter 7

The River War

A satisfied Winston stood in front of his tent at the 21st Lancers barracks in Cairo, Egypt. It was dawn on Wednesday, August 3, 1898. A short distance away he heard the shrill whistle of a river steamer and the stamping and snorting of Arabian stallions in their stalls onboard. It had taken eight months, but Winston had wrangled himself into another war. This time he was headed south into Sudan, attached to Major General Herbert Kitchener's Egyptian army. Just like the fighting in Malakand, the situation in Sudan had a long and twisted origin, rooted in Britain's determination to expand its empire around the world.

The Suez Canal, which was completed in 1869, bisected Egypt connecting the Mediterranean Sea with the Red Sea. It was built by the French and

Egyptians and financed by European banks. By 1875, Egypt's economy was in turmoil, and it could no longer make its promised payments to the banks. To avoid going bankrupt, the country sold its shares in the canal to the British. This suited the British, because the Suez Canal was the fastest route from Europe to India, an important trade route for them. Many Egyptians didn't like having British troops stationed along the canal, and tensions escalated to violent outbursts. In 1882, fearing that trade would be interrupted, the British army invaded and occupied Egypt, declaring it a de facto British protectorate.

As the situation in Egypt began to stabilize and the country's finances improved, the British governors turned their attention to the security of the Nile River. Egypt had only an inch of rainfall a year and relied completely on the Nile as its water supply. While Great Britain controlled the Nile as it flowed through Egypt, beyond its southern boundary the river flowed through Sudan. This presented two problems for the British. First, the French were threatening to take control of Sudan and dam the Nile before it reached Egypt, which would mean disaster for Egypt's people, agriculture, and industry. Second, Egypt controlled Sudan under the authority of the British, and during that time an insurrection had developed there. This was led by Mahdi Muhammad Ahmad, a Muslim leader who convinced tens of thousands of Sudanese tribesmen to follow him in revolt against their Egyptian overlords and establish the Caliphate of Omdurman.

These Sudanese tribes did not want to be governed by anyone, be they British or French. When British troops under the command of Colonel William Hicks had marched into Sudan in early November 1883 to quell the revolt, his force of eight thousand mostly Egyptian soldiers had been met by thousands of Sudanese tribesmen under the Mahdi's leadership. It was hard for Winston to contemplate what had happened next. Colonel Hicks's force had fought a pitched two-day battle with the Mahdist fighters. Only 250 of the colonel's men survived the battle. Colonel Hicks was among the dead. The result sent shockwaves through Great Britain.

Following the ill-fated battle, the British government decided to abandon Sudan to the Mahdists. They could not risk another battlefield slaughter. Yet there were still thousands of Egyptian soldiers, civilian employees, and their families still in Sudan. So British Major General Charles Gordon, widely known as Chinese Gordon, was sent to Khartoum, the Sudanese capital, to facilitate the evacuation of these people. Chinese Gordon appeared to be a good choice for the task, since he inspired confidence and was a national hero for his exploits on behalf of the British in China. However, Chinese Gordon didn't follow orders to evacuate everyone once he arrived in Khartoum. He evacuated the women and children but kept the Egyptian army units within the city walls. He envisioned leading a heroic attack against the Mahdists to regain lost territory. But things did not go as he imagined they would. In March 1884, Mahdist fighters surrounded Khartoum and besieged it. Charles Gordon and his troops survived for ten months before the Mahdists breached the city's wall on January 26, 1885. They swarmed into Khartoum. Major General Gordon was one of the ten thousand inhabitants killed in the city that day.

Winston was ten years old and attending St. George's School when he learned that Charles Gordon had been killed in Khartoum. The British public rallied around the quest to avenge Gordon's death at the hand of the Mahdists. Even Queen Victoria sent a telegram to the prime minister rebuking him for letting something like this happen to her beloved hero. Nine long years later, Major General Herbert Kitchener was given command of an Anglo-Egyptian army with orders to cross from Egypt into Sudan and deal with the Mahdist fighters once and for all.

Winston was sure the fight ahead would be fierce. He'd already heard reports of how fearless the Mahdi rebels were in battle, but he was certain the British would win. While their force consisted of eighty-two hundred British regular troops and a mixed group of seventeen thousand Sudanese and Egyptian soldiers, compared to the sixty thousand-strong Mahdi fighting force, the British were better armed. Not only did they have a fleet of armed gunboats to support them from the Nile, but also they had modern artillery pieces and the Maxim gun, a newly developed fully automatic machine gun that could fire off six hundred rounds a minute. Thanks to General Kitchener's methodical planning, the British had a secure support line to keep them supplied with everything they would need for the fight.

Breakfast was served as the sun rose over Cairo, after which it was time to get things loaded for the trip by paddle steamers up the Nile. The men of the 21st Lancers and local laborers loaded everything they required to wage war: trunks of uniforms, saddles, horse tack, picks, shovels, ammunition, dynamite, medical supplies, and thousands of pounds of food and horse fodder.

When the soldiers heard the all-aboard whistle they filed onto the paddle steamers. Winston stood on the foredeck of the steamer he was riding on as it cast off and drifted out into the Nile. The great paddle wheel slowly creaked into action, churning the river water into a muddy froth as it started its voyage upriver to Aswan.

Winston spent hours each day sitting under the awning on the boat's afterdeck. The Nile's current was swift, and the paddle steamers labored to make four miles an hour against it. This gave Winston plenty of time to take in the yellow desert that stretched to the horizon on both sides of the river. Date palms grew near the water, and small villages dotted the landscape, their mud huts giving off plumes of smoke from cooking fires. Sometimes small children waved from the riverbank. At sunset, the sky and land turned gold tinged with streaks of red and orange. When he wasn't gazing at the landscape, Winston wrote letters to family and friends or busily scribbled down notes about his impressions of things so far, to include in his newspaper articles. For reporting on this war, *The Morning Post* in London was paying him fifteen pounds per article.

It took a week to reach Aswan, where a series of rapids blocked the paddle steamers from going any farther upriver. The boats were unloaded, and the horses and camels exercised. Again, local laborers helped transport all the supplies six miles upriver past the rapids. There a different fleet of steamers awaited them to continue the journey up the Nile. Once again Winston was impressed. It took a lot of planning to move so many men, horses, and supplies in such an inhospitable land.

When the new boats were loaded and all the men and livestock were aboard, the steamers set off. Five days later, after crossing into Sudan, they arrived at Wadi Halfa. Here another set of rapids blocked their way, and the steamboats were unloaded again. This time, however, the freight was transferred to a military train that would carry them four hundred miles southeast to the staging camp at Atbara. After resting at Atbara for several days, Winston and the other four hundred members of the 21st Lancers set off on horseback while the others readied themselves to march to Omdurman.

On Thursday morning, September 1, 1898, Winston led a scouting party. Not long after leaving camp, they saw what looked like a huge black and white snake stretching across the hillside ahead. On closer inspection through his field glasses, Winston was surprised to see it was a long line of Mahdist fighters, some wearing white robes and the other dressed in black. More astonishingly, as the scouting party moved in for a closer look, Winston estimated that the line stretched on for five miles, moving forward in battle formation.

Colonel Rowland Martin, commander of the 21st Lancers, ordered Winston to report the situation to Major General Kitchener, whose army was set in battle formation about three miles away. Winston galloped off at full speed. The major general asked Winston how long he thought it would be before the Mahdist force reached them. Winston replied he thought it would take the Mahdists about an hour and a half to cover the ground. He bristled with excitement for the ensuing battle as he rode back to join the Lancers. However, at 2 p.m. the Mahdist force stopped and made camp. It appeared the battle would not take place that day after all.

That night a mixture of fear and anticipation permeated the Anglo-Egyptian camp. Winston found it hard to sleep. It wasn't so much the fear that kept him awake. He accepted that the chances were high he could be killed or wounded in the battle. What kept him awake was the excitement coursing through his body. Tomorrow would be the largest military fight he'd ever been a part of, and he wanted to experience it all.

At 4:30 a.m. the bugle sounded. Winston leapt from his cot to prepare for the day ahead. The men ate a hurried breakfast, and at 5:15 a.m. the 21st Lancers mounted their horses and rode out of camp. Winston and seven men were dispatched to ride ahead to spy on the Mahdists. The eight cavalrymen guided their horses to the top of a hill overlooking the Mahdist encampment. In the dim light of dawn,

Winston could see the vast array of enemy fighters already dressed and aligned for battle. There was no doubt—today was the day.

Winston scribbled his observations on paper and handed it to one of the other men. He instructed him to deliver the note to Major General Kitchener.

As the sun got brighter, Winston watched as the Anglo-Egyptian force assembled in battle position. Moments later the Mahdist fighters surged forward. They ran towards the Anglo-Egyptian army, their long robes billowing as they waved rifles and curved swords, their polished blades glinting in the early sunlight. Sitting on his horse above the valley where the battle was happening, Winston felt exactly like he had when as a boy he had arrayed regiments of lead soldiers and sent them into terrible battles. A trumpet sounded and the chatter-chat-chat sound filled the air as the Maxim guns burst to life. Mahdist fighters in the front line fell. The next row of men trampled over them as they surged forward.

Winston heard the pop of bullets close by. He turned to see Mahdist fighters storming up the hill. "Retreat. Find cover," he yelled as he reeled his horse around. As he galloped over the crest of the hill, what sounded like distant thunder filled the air. Major General Kitchener had ordered the British howitzers to open fire. Winston and his men found cover for themselves and their horses behind some large boulders, where they were well hidden. When he heard a cheer go up, Winston positioned himself to see what the fighters were doing. Having reached the top of the hill, the fighters waved black and white banners as they regrouped to surge down the other side of the hill and outflank the British. Winston knew that the waving banners would attract the attention of the British gunners, who would already be aiming their howitzer cannons on the rebels of the hill. Sure enough, as they began their charge down, the hill shook violently. The howitzer shells had found their mark. Winston could hear sickening screams above the thunder of the shells as Mahdist fighters were blown to pieces. As the howitzer shells continued to fall, Winston and his men knew they had to retreat quickly lest they were killed by friendly fire. As quickly as they could, they picked their way down the back side of the hill. Winston was relieved to rejoin the rest of the 21st Lancers to await further orders.

At 8:30 a.m. new orders came. Major General Kitchener wanted the men to mount a charge to clear a path through the Mahdist fighting line. This would allow an infantry column to march through the opening and on to the city of Omdurman. The Lancers aligned themselves in rows ready to charge, their long lances firmly positioned to take down the enemy. Since Winston couldn't carry a lance into battle because of his shoulder injury, he instead drew his pistol. As he steadied his horse, he focused on the fighters they were about to charge into. He estimated there were about five hundred of them.

When the bugles sounded, Winston dug his spurs into his horse's flank. The horse galloped forward. Within seconds, Winston was in the thick of things, the rhythmic thud of horse hooves upon the ground, the yelling of men, the crack of rifle fire, and the clanging of swords engulfed him. Winston kept pushing forward as the Lancers broke through the enemy line. He glanced right and left. All his comrades seemed to be accounted for. On the ground, dozens of Mahdist fighters lay dead or wounded. Winston assumed the rest would meld back into the barren landscape. Surely, they could see that on foot they wouldn't prevail against the British cavalry. In a flash, Winston caught sight of a huge swell of men clad in black and white. They had been obscured from view in a slight depression in the ground. At least three thousand or more were standing fourteen deep in some places and surging forward. It was impossible to turn back now. The Lancers would have to face this new wave of fighters head on. Back at full gallop they crashed into the Mahdists. Chaos was everywhere as lances were thrust, swords swung, and guns popped. Their eyes wild, horses buckled under their riders as Mahdist fighters slashed at their legs. Winston knew the only thing to do was keep moving. If he faltered or his horse fell, he was a dead man. On he went until at last he once again broke through the enemy line. The Lancers then reeled their horses ready for another charge, but this time the Mahdists were on the run. Winston breathed a sigh of relief.

The men of the 21st Lancers dismounted to tend to their dead and injured comrades. They draped wounded men over their saddles and transported them to the field hospital. They shot several horses to put them out of their agony. They gathered the dead bodies. They also tallied up the cost of their charge. Of the three hundred ten Lancers involved in the charge, twenty-one had been killed and forty-nine were wounded. One hundred nineteen horses were dead.

By mid-afternoon, the Battle of Omdurman was over. The Anglo-Egyptian force had captured the city of Omdurman and crossed the Nile to secure Khartoum, the capital of Sudan. The goals of the Anglo-Egyptian force had been accomplished. Sudan was now back under British control, and the death of Major General Charles Gordon had been avenged. Soldiers would soon be dispatched to hunt down and pacify the thirty thousand rebel fighters who had slipped away. The British army's superior weapons and a professional fighting force had won the day. Twelve thousand Mahdi fighters lay dead strewn among the desert rocks, five thousand were taken prisoner, and an indeterminate number had been wounded. By contrast, a total of nearly four hundred members of the Anglo-Egyptian force had been wounded and forty-eight killed.

The next day Winston felt torn as he walked the field of combat. The battle had showcased the latest weaponry—howitzers, Maxim guns, and modern rifles against which the Mahdist fighters never stood a chance. Winston had felt exhilarated during the cavalry charge, but now, surveying the carnage he was appalled by what he saw. While the British and Egyptian bodies had already been buried and the injured transferred to field hospitals, the wounded Mahdists were left writhing in pain until they died.

Yes, Winston thought, *these Mahdist fighters were enemy combatants, but they were also human beings.* They needed help and compassion, but Major General Kitchener had instructed his men to ignore them.

Following the Battle of Omdurman, the 21st Lancers were stood down. Winston returned with them to Cairo, and then in October he returned to England. His book *The Story of the Malakand Field Force* had been published and many important people were reading and commenting on it. Spurred on by the book's popularity, Winston gathered his field notes along with the articles he'd sent to the newspaper. He began to write an account of his recent experiences on the Nile.

While in London writing the book that he had titled *The River War,* Winston thought long and hard about his future. He had participated in three different military campaigns in Cuba, North-West India, and Sudan. And although the experiences had filled him with excitement, they had also left him with disdain for the barbarity of war. It was nothing like the pretend battles he had played with his toy soldiers where he could pick them up and set them back in place when he was done. In real battles, hundreds, maybe thousands, of men on both sides were killed or maimed for life.

Winston decided it was time for him to move on from the military and pursue his goal of being a politician like his father and grandfather before him. To do that he had to return to the 4th Queen's Own Hussars in Bangalore and resign his commission.

He also had another aim he wanted to achieve before leaving the army. Winston was determined to play in the inter-regimental polo tournament of 1899. No polo team from a regiment based in South India had ever won the tournament, and Winston was sure that a team from the Hussars would be the first to do so.

Chapter 8

An Offer He Couldn't Refuse

On December 2, 1898, Winston set out for India again to resign his commission and help the 4th Queen's Own Hussars win the 1899 inter-regimental polo tournament. It took him three months to accomplish both. He even scored the final, winning goal in the inter-regimental polo match, despite having his arm strapped to his chest because of his old shoulder injury. Nearly three years had passed since Winston stood in the lighter boat coming ashore in Bombay. Now it was time for him to return to England and see what kind of politician he could become.

Winston arrived back in London in April 1899. Within days of returning his last remaining grandparent, the Dowager Duchess of Marlborough, died. Winston was glad to be there to support his mother.

Following the funeral, the will was read. To Winston's dismay he learned that his grandmother had cut him, Jack, and their mother out of her will.

It came as a shock to them all. Winston was grateful he no longer had to bear the cost of maintaining his horses, and leaving the army was saving him a lot of money. Jack, who worked for a stockbroker in London, had been hoping to use his inheritance to attend university. Now he would have to stay in his current job. Winston knew that his mother would struggle to continue living the high life. She'd already borrowed money against her now evaporated inheritance and had no way to pay it back. Marrying a rich man seemed like a sensible course of action, but Winston's mother was anything but sensible when it came to matters of the heart. She promptly fell in love with George Cornwallis-West, an officer in the Scots Guards. George was just two weeks older than Winston and Winston tried not to dwell too much on his mother's love affair.

That summer, Winston began speaking at Conservative Party meetings at fairs, marketplaces, and meeting halls. Drawing on the oratory advice Bourke Cockran had given him in New York City, Winston worked hard honing his speeches. He discovered he could hold an audience spellbound. He loved the combination of nervousness beforehand and exhilaration afterwards. Before long he was selected as one of the party's two parliamentary candidates for the June 1899 by-election in Oldham, Lancashire. Despite his best effort, Winston narrowly lost the election to the Liberal Party candidate. While disappointed, he was sure that he would do better next time—convinced that his future lay in politics.

Meanwhile, tensions were boiling over in Southern Africa. The first Dutch settlers who had arrived there in the late seventeenth and early eighteenth centuries, were known as Boers. They were soon joined by the British, who quickly formed the British Cape Colony where the Boers had settled. After 1836 many Boers, unhappy with British rule, decided to migrate east away from the British Cape Colony. About fifteen thousand people departed to the eastern coast, where they established the Republic of Natalia. However, in 1843 Great Britain once again moved into Boer territory, annexed the republic, and renamed it Natal. The Boers then moved again, this time northwards into South Africa's interior, and established two new independent republics, which they named the Transvaal Republic and the Orange Free State. Great Britain begrudgingly recognized the two new republics.

As a boy, Winston had learned all about this in history classes at school. However, things were now even more tense between Great Britain and the Boers. During the 1880s diamonds and gold were discovered in the area the Boers controlled. As a result of these newfound riches, the British tried to wrestle control of the two republics from them. But the Boers resisted, and now it looked like the two sides were headed towards war.

Soon after Winston had sent off the manuscript of *The River War* to his publisher in September 1899, he received an offer he couldn't refuse. *The Morning*

Post newspaper in London offered him 250 pounds a month for at least four months to be their principal war correspondent in South Africa. All his expenses would also be covered. Winston accepted the offer without hesitation. The timing was perfect. Not only would he earn good money, but also he would be able for a while to escape England and all the questions he was being asked about his mother and George Cornwallis-West, who had just created a scandal by announcing their engagement.

At twenty-four years old, Winston was on his way to his fourth combat zone. This time though, he wouldn't have military officers directing him. He would be free to roam at will and poke his nose wherever he wanted.

On October 11, 1899, the British gave the Boers a deadline to either stand down from their resistance or expect an attack. Winston believed it would be suicide for the Boers to continue resisting, since their entire population was less than one hundred thousand and most of the people were poor farmers. They could not win against the might of the British army with 450,000 men from across the empire at its disposal.

Three days later, Winston sailed for South Africa aboard the RMS *Dunottar Castle*, not knowing whether or not the Boers had accepted the British ultimatum. Also traveling aboard ship was General Sir Redvers Buller and many senior army officers. They too were desperate to know if, when they reached South Africa, they were headed into a war or about to negotiate a peace treaty. Winston couldn't think of a worse time to be out of contact with the outside world, and he didn't expect to know anything until the ship docked in Madeira four days later. But when the *Dunottar Castle* reached Madeira the only news to be had was that both sides were on the move. Winston and everyone else aboard would have to wait until they reached Cape Town, South Africa. In the meantime, the ship would steam down the coast of the French Congo, Portuguese West Africa, German South West Africa and on until they reached the southern tip of the African continent.

On the tenth day of sailing, a small tramp steamer appeared on the horizon. Winston hoped the vessel might have news of what was happening in South Africa. The *Dunottar Castle's* signalman semaphored to request any news. The tramp steamer maneuvered to within a hundred yards of their ship, until the message written on a blackboard on her deck became clearly visible: "BOERS DEFEATED. THREE BATTLES. PENN SYMONDS KILLED."

The seven words of the message were the source of endless debates aboard, right until the *Dunottar Castle* dropped anchored in Table Bay, Cape Town. While it was close to midnight, launches quickly ferried military experts aboard to consult with General Buller and his staff. Winston questioned as many of them as he could. The news he received was grim. The Boers had not surrendered. They were fighting back. They now had the British towns of Mafeking and Kimberley surrounded, and Ladysmith in Natal was under threat. The blackboard message on the tramp steamer had given everyone aboard the *Dunottar Castle* false hope. The Boers were certainly not defeated.

Armed with this news and the fact that it would take Commander in Chief Sir Redvers Buller at least a month to set up his headquarters, Winston determined to go on ahead to Ladysmith. This required a seven-hundred-mile train trip east to Port Elizabeth and a mail boat journey from there to Durban, the closest port to Ladysmith. With any luck he could make the journey in four days.

When he arrived in Durban, Winston learned that he was too late to get to Ladysmith. The Boers had surrounded the town, which was under siege. Nonetheless, he decided to get as close to the action as possible. He took a train inland to Estcourt, thirty-five miles south of Ladysmith.

Once he arrived in Estcourt, Winston learned that an armored train was frequently sent north about ten to fifteen miles towards Ladysmith to see whether the Boers were advancing in their direction. The train was under the command of Captain Aylmer Haldane, someone Winston knew from his days in India. Captain Haldane invited Winston to come along on one of the train forays so that he could write about it. Winston boarded the armored train at 5:10 a.m. on the morning of Wednesday, November 15, 1899, to travel the fifteen miles up the track.

The steam locomotive was situated in the middle of the train. In front of it were a flat truck and the troop carriage. Mounted to the open flat truck was a seven-pounder gun manned by men of HMS *Tartar*. Winston climbed aboard the front troop carriage, which had sides made of thick plate steel. It had no roof, just slots in the steel walls to fire rifles through. Behind the steam engine was a coal tender, followed by two more armored carriages filled with soldiers. The last carriage was a flat bogie wagon on which any necessary equipment to repair the railway line was loaded. In all, Winston was one of 120 armed men on the train.

The train reached the station in Frere without incident. Captain Haldane talked to some policemen who were patrolling the area. They reported that all was clear to go on to the next stop, Chieveley. Along the way, Winston got his first view of the Boers through the rifle slots in the carriage wall. In the distance a wagon train with about fifty Boers was headed west. The train made it to Chieveley without encountering any more Boers. However, the station-master told them there were reports of Boer militias nearby. Captain Haldane ordered the train to back down the track towards Frere as quickly as possible. Winston's pulse quickened. Were they about to encounter real action? He hoped so.

The train was about two miles from Frere when a lookout gave a shout. He had spotted several hundred Boers on a ridge eight hundred yards to the west. There was another shout. A line of Boers appeared to the east. Captain Haldane ordered his soldiers to open fire. Within seconds Winston heard the unmistakable clatter of a Maxim machine gun and a hail of bullets slamming against the steel sides of the carriage. Suddenly with a jolt, the train shook violently and came to an abrupt stop. Winston and most of the other soldiers were thrown to the floor.

Winston picked himself up and scrambled for the door. He had to see what was happening outside. He glanced back at the flat truck with the seven-pounder gun on it. Men were preparing to fire it as bullets rained down. Winston ran along the track. The steam engine and coal tender, along with the front carriage, were still coupled and upright, but beyond the tender was chaos. Bleeding, dazed men clambered over twisted metal. Winston dodged around them until he could see the cause of the mayhem. A large boulder lay on the tracks, and it had caused the three back carriages to derail. It was obviously put there by the Boers to stop the train. It hadn't been on the track when they passed this spot on the trip up to Chieveley. Suddenly Winston heard a loud boom. He turned to see the front truck with the seven-pounder gun explode, hit by a round from a Boer cannon. The scene was choking in smoke, bodies, and chaos. Winston knew there wasn't a second to waste. They were sitting ducks waiting for the Boers to pick them off. They had to get the derailed carriages off the track so the rest of the train passengers could escape before they were all killed.

Instinctively, Winston sprang into action. He sprinted back to the steam locomotive. Both the driver and the fireman crouched beside their engine as bullets flew. The driver's face was covered in blood, but he was too dazed to notice. "Get back into the engine," Winston yelled. "We have to move the train now." Neither man budged. It was as if they were in a trance. Winston changed tactics. "Let's move this train," he said and, pointing to the driver's bloodied face, added, "Don't worry. You can't be hit by a bullet twice in one day. You'll be fine now. Let's get moving. Stoke the engine, and I'll clear the carriages away from the tracks behind us. As soon as I give the word, we'll be out of here. Up you go." The two men stared at Winston for a moment, then obediently climbed back aboard the locomotive cab.

Winston ignored the flying bullets as he yelled for men to help him clear the tracks. About fifteen soldiers emerged from behind the wreckage. "The rock first," Winston yelled. The men swarmed around it. Those in front put their shoulders against the boulder and pushed while those behind them lowered their shoulders and pushed the men. They were like a rugby scrum moving against the rock. At last the boulder moved. The men pushed harder until it rolled off the track.

"To the carriage," Winston yelled. The men moved to the next obstacle. The flat bogie wagon at the end of the train had flipped upon impact with the boulder and now lay upside down on the embankment and off the track. The troop carriage attached to it was also upside down and off the track. But the next troop carriage, while still on its wheels, sat sideways across the track. The men tried to move it, but its steel sides made it too heavy to budge. It would have to be shunted out of the way with the locomotive. To help it maneuver more easily, Winston uncoupled the front carriages and then raced to the engine. He climbed into the cab. Bellowing above the clatter of guns he told the driver, "The rock is gone, and two of the carriages are clear of the tracks. But we'll have to shunt the last troop carriage aside to get through. Let's do it." With that he jumped down from the cab to direct the operation.

Winston waved at the engine driver. The locomotive shuddered and moved. The sound of grinding metal filled the air as it rammed into the carriage. It moved, but not enough. "Go forward and try again," Winston yelled to the engine driver. It felt like a bullet-riddled eternity to Winston, but after three tries the locomotive bashed the stubborn troop carriage aside and slipped past it.

The locomotive and coal tender were free, but for how long? Everyone around now understood Winston's plan. They dragged wounded men up on top of the coal piled in the tender and lay others on the cowcatcher wherever there was room. Other wounded soldiers were placed on top of the locomotive's boiler. And one dazed man clung to the smokestack. Winston jumped into the engine cab and encouraged the driver to ease the train back slowly, slow enough that the soldiers on the ground outside could continue to return fire at the Boers while using the locomotive for cover as they retreated from the ambush.

As the train backed up, the Boers closed in on the railway line. Winston glanced out the cab window to see Captain Haldane sprinting forward past the engine, headed towards a small group of soldiers who'd been left behind. Winston leapt from the locomotive cab to help the captain rescue them. Meanwhile the train increased its speed lest the surging Boers catch up to it.

Before Winston reached the men left behind, he saw two of them waving white handkerchiefs. They were surrendering. Winston was shocked. They'd all had a good chance of making it back to the train and safety, but it was too late now. Winston had no intention of surrendering. He swerved to the side, raced up the embankment, and dived into a ditch for cover. His heart pounded as he saw the other soldiers drop their weapons and raise their hands. Winston then heard the click of a gun being cocked. He looked up to see the barrel of a rifle aimed at him. There was no way out. He could cooperate or be shot. Winston raised his hands to surrender. He was marched back to join the other captives. To his left he could see the locomotive with the tender puffing its way back down the track, men clinging from it. Winston knew his quick thinking had saved many lives, but at a cost. He was now a prisoner of war.

Chapter 9

Wanted...Dead or Alive

The following day, Winston was marched past the town of Ladysmith with the other fifty-two British captives on a sixty-mile trek to Elandslaagte, where they were put on a train to the Boer's capital—Pretoria.

Three days after being captured, Winston arrived in Pretoria. Stepping off the train there, the captives were divided into two groups, enlisted men on one side, officers on the other. Winston was the only reporter among them, and he was grouped with the officers. The officers formed a line and were marched through Pretoria to their prisoner of war camp. As they marched through the gate, it was easy to see the place had once been a school. There were rows of classrooms and a yard in the middle, but some things were different. Two sides of the compound were enclosed with an eight-foot-high iron fence with spikes on top. The other two sides were bounded by a ten-foot-high sturdy wooden and corrugated iron fence. Most of the courtyard was taken up with tents, not for the captives but for the sixty guards who ran and patrolled the compound.

For the first week, Winston found daily life as a prisoner of war interesting. It was an aspect of war he'd never encountered before and had its own rhythm. He slept in a converted classroom. The men were free to roam wherever they wanted any time of the day or night. They were allowed to buy or barter for newspapers, cigars, food, even beer from the Boers. He imagined this was because they were all officers and not enlisted men. Of course, they couldn't leave the prison compound. Ten armed Boer soldiers were always on sentry duty, seven patrolling inside the fence and three outside.

During the following week, Winston noticed that some of his fellow prisoners adapted quite well. The men held chess tournaments and formed a book club. But Winston refused to adapt himself to prison life. He was a reporter, not a soldier, and felt that he should be released immediately. The camp commandant disagreed. Winston prowled around the prison camp in a foul mood. He hated being couped up with his fate in the hands of others. He needed action, even foolhardy action, he concluded, would be better than sitting out the rest of the war as a prisoner.

Winston saw his chance when he overheard Captain Aylmer Haldane and Sergeant Brockie hatching an escape plan. He interrupted them, glad to find two officers ready to act. Captain Haldane explained that he and Sergeant Brockie were thinking of climbing out of a bathroom window. Winston knew which one immediately—the high window in the bathroom that abutted one of the corrugated iron fences. Once they had climbed through the window and dropped to the ground, they could scale the corrugated iron fence, slip into the garden of the house on the other side, and make their way out into the street. Captain Haldane explained that when it was dark, despite the electric floodlights, that part of the outside wall was in the shadows. And at the point where the bathroom was located, the night guards would turn their backs to each other and walk in opposite directions as they patrolled. If everything went to plan, there was just enough time for a man to climb out the window and scale the fence while the guards were both marching in the opposite direction.

"And what happens once you make it into the street?" Winston asked.

'We find the train track and jump on a freight train heading east," Captain Haldane said. "It's about three hundred miles from here to neutral Portuguese East Africa."

Winston nodded. "Can I go with you?" he asked.

Captain Haldane and Sergeant Brockie looked at each other silently, and then each man nodded his head. Winston let out a sigh of relief.

"This place is intolerable. I can't sit out the rest of the war here," Winston said. "Let's make our escape attempt tomorrow evening." Captain Haldane and Sergeant Brockie nodded.

It was a risky plan, Winston knew, but it was better than anything he'd come up with. Besides, they had an advantage. Sergeant Brockie spoke Afrikaans, and Captain Haldane had a compass and a local map he'd cut out of a book in the library.

The next day, December 12, four weeks after being captured as a prisoner of war, Winston bartered for a brown suit from another prisoner. He stuffed his pockets with four bars of chocolate, a few biscuits, and seventy-five pounds in cash. He had also written a letter addressed to the camp commandant and left it on his bunk. In the letter he declared, "I have the honour to inform you that as I do not consider that your Government has any right to detain me as a military prisoner, I have decided to escape from your custody."

Later that evening, Winston walked casually towards the bathroom. He spotted Captain Haldane in the prison courtyard. Their eyes met, and the captain nodded slightly. Everything was in place. The plan was for Winston to be the first to climb out of the bathroom window. When the sentries turned their backs to the bathroom and marched away from each other, Winston scrambled through the window and dropped silently to the ground. He then leveraged himself between the brick wall of the bathroom and the corrugated iron perimeter fence and climbed over the fence into the adjacent garden.

Everything had gone as planned. Winston crouched behind a camelia bush and waited for the other two men to drop down beside him. Minutes ticked by, but neither man climbed over the wall.

Winston waited longer. Still, no one came over the wall. He began to ponder his situation. There was no way he could climb back over the wall into the prison. There was nothing on the garden side he could use for leverage, and he was sure he would be spotted by the guards if he tried. After waiting still longer, Winston finally concluded the other two men had aborted the mission. Perhaps the sentries had unexpectedly changed their routine. He didn't know. All he knew was that he was now on his own and needed to get as far away from the prison as quickly as possible.

Winston moved cautiously out from behind the shrubbery, then out the gate and into the street. He fell into step behind a group of men on the street. He forced himself to put his hands in his pocket and whistle as he walked, but his mind raced with questions. What should he do next? He had three hundred miles to cover, a near impossible challenge, since he did not have either Sergeant Brockie's knowledge of Afrikaans to rely on or the map and compass Captain Haldane was carrying. As he walked on, Winston heard a train whistle and realized he was near the railway line. That was the answer. He would hop on a freight train as they had planned and use the sun and stars to guide him in the right direction. Hopefully he would find some food and water along the way.

Winston clambered down beside the railway track, and before long the track began to vibrate. He could hear the rumble of an approaching train—a freight train! This was his chance. As the train slowed to negotiate a curve, Winston ran alongside it. Finding a handhold for the train car in the moonlight turned out to be harder than he expected. On his third try he succeeded and pulled himself aboard. He soon found himself in an open truck filled with piles of empty coal sacks. *Perfect*, he thought, as he pulled some sacks over his body. No one would spot him now.

Winston settled in and ate a chocolate bar. He wondered how long he should stay on the train. The more he thought about it, the more convinced he became that he should travel at night and rest during the day. At daybreak he leapt from the train. He found a stream nearby and drank heartily from it. It felt good to clear the coal dust from his throat. He found a hiding place that gave him a good view of his surroundings. He stayed hidden all day watching trains chug by. In the distance he saw a train station, with a steep incline leading away from it, causing the trains to slow down there. Winston decided that was the perfect place to hop on another freight train. At sunset he headed towards the station, being careful to stay in the shadows.

It was dark by the time he skirted the station and found an obscure place to wait for a passing train. Several hours later, Winston gave up. *Perhaps trains traveled through this area only during the day*, he thought. He was hungry and dejected and ate another chocolate bar.

As the last square of chocolate melted in his mouth, Winston noticed a distant light. Was it a fire? A campfire perhaps. He started walking towards it.

As he got closer, he saw that he was approaching a coal mine, the fire was in its boiler. There was also a two-story stone cottage and several outbuildings at the mine. Winston hid behind a bush to think. He wasn't sure what to do next. He needed food, but he was deep in Boer territory. If he tried to rouse someone in the cottage, that person would surely sound the alarm. Then he remembered hearing back in the prison camp in Pretoria that several of the coal mines in the area were run by Englishmen. The Boers wouldn't let them leave because they were experts in managing mines. Winston had a choice to make: did he take the gamble and knock, or did he keep on walking?

He took a deep breath, stepped out from behind the bush, and walked up to the cottage door. He knocked, his heart beating wildly. His freedom hinged upon who opened the door. Moments later he heard a voice from an upper story window demand, "Wer ist da?" Winston's heart sank. The man spoke Afrikaans.

Winston's mind raced. What could he say? He had to make something up. "I need help. I have had an accident," he replied and waited. He heard footsteps inside, and then the front door swung open.

A tall man in a dressing gown glared at him. "Well, what do you want?" he asked again, this time in perfect English.

"I'm Winston Churchill," he introduced himself.

The man grunted. "Yes, no doubt you are. We've had people asking about you all day. Come in." He opened the door wider and stepped back.

Within minutes, Winston was sitting at a table enjoying a meat sandwich and a hot cup of tea. He learned that his host was John Howard, a dual citizen of Great Britain and Transvaal and manager of the Transvaal Collieries. John also told Winston there were four other British citizens at the colliery. Winston was almost positive that John would not hand him over to the authorities, so he described how he'd escaped and gotten this far.

"Well, we'll see what we can do to get you on your way," John said as Winston slathered butter onto another piece of bread. "You'll have to give me a little time to put things together, but I think it might be possible."

"Thank you," Winston replied with a nod, knowing that John Howard was taking a big risk. Harboring a fugitive during wartime was a serious offense.

"You can't stay in the house. My housekeeper is a Boer," John warned. He tapped his fingers on the table and then said, "I think the best thing is to hide you inside the mine. You're not afraid of tight spaces, are you?"

"No," Winston said, wondering just how tight the space might be.

John stood and picked up a basket. "Let me put a few things together for you and then we'll pay a call on Dan Dewsnap. He's a Scot who'd be more than happy to outwit the Boers," he said with a chuckle.

Within half an hour of knocking on the cottage door, Winston was in his new hiding place behind a pile of rocks in the bottom of the mine. Two Scotsmen had guided him down there, taking a thin mattress and blanket with them. They also carried a basket of supplies John had gathered, including more sandwiches, a packet of biscuits, and several apples, along with a box of cigars, matches, and candles, plus a flagon of water and an enamel cup. Winston could hardly believe his luck. He'd found one of the few people in Transvaal willing and able to help him.

Time passed slowly below ground. Winston read by candlelight and kicked at the rats who scampered around his food basket. All he could do was wait for someone to come for him. Even if he wanted to, Winston doubted he could find the way to the surface.

After two days John appeared in the mine and led Winston up to his house. "The plan is nearly in place. You'll need to stay in here," he said, opening the door to a storeroom. Winston stepped inside. The place was piled high with files and ledger books. "Look at this," John said, holding up a newspaper. On the front page was a photo of Winston in uniform. John translated the text into English from Afrikaans. "Wanted Winston Churchill. Twenty-five pounds reward for the capture, dead or alive." Winston wasn't surprised. "They think you're still in Pretoria. Since you arrived here no one's been by to ask about you."

John brought Winston a bowl of soup and some toast. "I'm going to have to lock you in here. The housekeeper doesn't have a key, so keep quiet," he said after Winston had finished eating. He pointed at some books on the desk and added, "Something else for you to read."

The next evening John returned with more food and a plan. "I have a friend here who's a farmer and is about to ship some bales of wool by train over the border to Lourenço Marques. We're going to put you on that train. The bales will be loaded on at our siding, so we will have control over who sees what. We'll slip you onto a wagon, and we'll leave a gap so that you can worm your way back into the middle of the bales. Then we'll cover the whole wagon with a tarpaulin. Hopefully, the border guards won't bother lifting it and you'll make it across safely into Portuguese territory.

"When can I go?" Winston asked.

"Two days' time," John replied. "I think it's going to work. Sometimes the border guards inspect the bales of wool, but not all the time."

Winston nodded. "Thank you for all you are doing for me."

Two days later, John appeared again. He checked to see that no one was watching and then walked Winston from the storeroom to the siding. "There," he said, pointing to a space between two wool bales. "We've left a bigger gap for you inside. Take this, and good luck." He handed Winston a knapsack. Then the two men shook hands. Winston climbed between the bales of wool and slid down until he came to the gap in the center of the rail wagon. It was big enough to sit down in. Soon he felt the wagon lurch forward. He settled in for the trip ahead.

Two and a half days later the train came to a stop. Winston could hear heaving and grunting and the sound of men talking. His heart thumped as their voices got closer to his hiding place. Winston listened. The men were speaking Portuguese, not Afrikaans. Relief flooded through him. He'd made it to safety.

Even so, Winston didn't want to break his cover yet. He waited an hour until everything was quiet before crawling out and climbing to the ground. He was in a shunting yard. He stretched his stiff limbs, then headed towards the town. He needed to find the British consul's office in Lourenço Marques as quickly as possible.

Winston found the consul's office without any difficulty, though the gatekeeper didn't want to let him in. He knew he looked a sight. On his way to the office, he learned it was December 21. Nine days had passed since his escape from Pretoria, and he was still wearing the same clothes. Winston had to get inside the building. He yelled until the consul himself came to see what the problem was.

Everything was soon sorted out, and Winston was ushered inside and served a hearty meal. As Winston ate, the consul explained that while Winston was in hiding, things had gone badly for the British. So badly, in fact, the week of December 10–17 had been dubbed "Black Week." During this time the British had lost three battles at Stromberg, Magersfontein, and Colenso. As a result, twenty-seven hundred British soldiers had been killed, wounded, or captured. Winston could scarcely believe it. The Boers were tenacious fighters.

After he had eaten, Winston enjoyed a hot bath and changed into a new set of clothes provided by the consul.

By then a crowd had gathered outside the consulate. British men living in Lourenço Marques had gathered to escort Winston to the docks and board a boat headed for British territory. The consul explained that Winston was not safe in Lourenço Marques. Many in the city sympathized with the Boers, and he could easily be captured and sent back across the border for the reward money. Winston stepped through the gate and was immediately surrounded by the men, who walked in a group down to the docks and stood around him while he bought a ticket. They then walked him onboard the *Induna*, which was bound for Durban. Winston stood on deck and waved at the men on the dock. Tears filled his eyes. He owed his safety to them and so many others.

Two days later the *Induna* steamed into Durban's harbor. Winston was surprised to see the large crowd that had gathered on the dock waving Union Jack flags. As the gangway was hoisted into place, a band began to play. It was some kind of celebration, but for who or what? Winston watched as the crowd parted, allowing three men, two in military uniforms, to reach the gangplank, which they strode up. "Winston Churchill?" one of them yelled as they stepped aboard ship. Winston stepped forward. The man, whose uniform Winston now recognized as that of an admiral, thrust out his hand. "It is an honor to welcome back a national hero!" he said. A cheer went up from the crowd.

Winston was shocked. He wasn't aware that people had been alerted to the fact that he was onboard.

Once on the dock, Winston felt himself being hoisted onto some men's shoulders. The crowd carried him to the steps of the town hall. The mayor of Durban welcomed Winston and then gave a speech. He told Winston that because of his bravery and quick thinking during the train ambush, many soldiers had made it back alive. That, along with his daring escape from the prisoner of war camp in Pretoria, had made Winston a household name in Durban and in Great Britain.

That night, after dining with city dignitaries, Winston received his mail. He learned that his brother Jack had signed up for the South African Light Horse Brigade and was on his way to South Africa. In another letter he learned that his cousin Sunny was also coming to serve as assistant military secretary to Lord Frederick Roberts, the newly appointed Commander in Chief Field Marshall. His mother wrote to say that her fiancé George Cornwallis-West, a lieutenant in the Scots Guards, was also enroute to South Africa and that she had founded a charity that raised over forty thousand dollars to outfit a hospital ship.

Winston chuckled as he read that his mother was about to sail for Cape Town aboard the newly refitted S.S. *Maine*. Winston was sure his mother's efforts would be seen as a bright spot in a war where victory had not been as fast or smooth as predicted. Everyone had anticipated that the fighting would be over by Christmas, but that wasn't the case. As the dawn of a new century approached, the Boers showed no sign of giving up.

By Christmas Eve Winston was back where it all started. He was camped about one hundred yards from where the ambush of the train had taken place. The crosses in the red dirt beside the railway track reminded him of the men who had lost their lives that day. Ladysmith, twenty-two miles up the track, was still under siege and the British high command were desperate to relieve the town. It had been under siege for fifty-five days by now, and there were reports that all the animals had been slaughtered and eaten and there was little food left.

On January 6, 1900, Winston was questioned by General Buller about his time in captivity in Pretoria. The general wanted to know if there was anything he'd seen or heard while there that might help them capture the city. When the debrief was over, the general asked Winston if there was anything he could do for him. This was music to Winston's ears. He did want one thing. Winston longed to do his duty as a commissioned officer once more and inquired whether the general would allow that. After a long pause, General Buller granted Winston's request with the understanding that he wouldn't draw pay for doing so. Winston agreed immediately, delighted to be assigned an adjutant-assistant to Colonel Julian Byng of the South African Light Horse Brigade.

Within days, Winston was back in uniform. His first assignment was scouting and running dispatches at the Battle of Spion Kopje, where the British were trying to capture a prominent hilltop where the Boers were entrenched. They needed to take the hilltop so they could bring in cannons to protect

British infantry as they marched to Ladysmith. The battle took place on January 23–24, 1900, and ended in another British defeat. Nearly 250 British soldiers were killed and 1,250 wounded, with the hilltop still controlled by the Boers. Winston began to have doubts about General Buller's leadership ability. The general didn't seem to have a good grip on tactical maneuvers.

A week after the defeat at Spion Kopje, Winston was granted three days' leave to travel to Durban for the arrival of his mother aboard the SS *Maine.* The ship had picked up Jack in Cape Town.

It was wonderful to be together again. Winston marveled at the way his mother had seamlessly swapped her fine silk gowns for a starched white uniform with a red cross armband and went by the name Sister Jennie. Yet her role aboard was not as nurse but as administrator. She seemed to know everyone and everything that was going on aboard the ship.

Following the visit to the SS *Maine,* Winston returned to the South African Light Horse Brigade with Jack in tow. For the first time, the Churchill brothers fought side by side. They were involved in four attempts to break through the Boer lines to relieve the siege of Ladysmith. These attempts involved British forces crossing the Tugela River and attacking Boer positions as they tried to break through their lines and relieve the town. Each time, the British forces were defeated and had to retreat to the south side of the Tugela River. During the fourth attack, a bullet ripped through Jack's leg. Winston helped him onto an ambulance wagon. After the battle, Winston dashed off a note to his mother warning her that Jack was on his way—as a patient.

Eventually the tide began to turn in the military struggle. The British captured Monte Cristo Range from the Boers. This in turn, allowed them to capture the town of Colenso on the south bank of the Tugela River and build a pontoon bridge across it. From there they pushed towards Ladysmith. The Boers retreated, and after 121 days the siege of the town was over. Winston rode into Ladysmith on March 1, 1900, one of the proudest moments of his life.

With the relief of Ladysmith accomplished and with the Boers in retreat, the British marched northwest into the Boer country of Transvaal. They captured Johannesburg and marched north towards Pretoria, which they occupied on June 5, 1900. It was a sweet moment for Winston as he rode alongside Sunny into Pretoria. Things had come full circle. He had escaped the prisoner of war camp there and now had returned to liberate those who had been left behind.

Following the capture of Pretoria, it appeared the war was all but over. It was time for Winston to focus on his future. He'd found fame as a war correspondent and escaped as a prisoner of war. Now it was time to return to Great Britain and concentrate on his political career. This time around he was determined to win a seat in the House of Commons.

Chapter 10

A Winning Formula

On July 4, 1900, Winston Churchill boarded the *Dunottar Castle* for the trip home. His mother had already left aboard the SS *Maine* with a contingent of wounded soldiers. Jack had made a good recovery and rejoined the South African Light Horse regiment to "mop up" the end of the war.

Winston spent much of the sixteen-day return voyage editing his newspaper dispatches and writing an account of his capture and escape. He planned to call the book *Ian Hamilton's March*.

A week after Winston arrived home, his mother married George Cornwallis-West at St. Paul's Church in Knightsbridge, London. While Winston liked George, he found it impossible to think of him as a stepfather—the two men were the same age. Many people called the marriage between the two a scandal.

Queen Victoria struck Jennie Churchill from her roster of woman she invited to tea, the military fired George, and his father all but disinherited him.

While his mother and George were honeymooning in France, Winston ran for a seat in the House of Commons as a conservative. The Conservative Party, which currently controlled the Commons, stood for traditional upper-class values—Queen, Church, and Empire. The other main political party, the Liberals, appealed to the middle and lower classes and was more interested in providing a good education for everyone, labor laws, and ways in which to alleviate the grinding poverty that existed in many British towns and cities.

Winston was offered other seats to run for, but he stayed with Oldham, where he had narrowly lost in the previous election. It was a predominantly liberal electorate, but Winston hoped his fame and personality would win over voters in the district. The challenge appealed to him.

Winston campaigned hard and won by twenty-two votes. The local elections for members of the House of Commons were staggered over a six-week period, with Oldham's being one of the first. Having demonstrated his ability to win, Winston was immediately in demand campaigning for conservative candidates in other areas. He wrote to Bourke Cockran in New York City to say, "I have suddenly become one of the two or three most popular speakers in this election....great audiences (five and six thousand people) twice & even three times a day, bands, crowds and enthusiasm of all kinds."

Winston was particularly amused when a group of mill girls made up a ditty about him:

You've heard of Winston Churchill;
This is all I need to say—
He's the latest and the greatest
Correspondent of the day.

In November, when the national election results were tallied, the Conservative Party had the majority in Parliament by a solid margin.

The excitement was over, and now Winston had to find a way to pay for the privilege of being a member of the House of Commons. The position didn't come with a salary, and each member had to pay his own way or find a sponsor. His cousin Sunny, who sat as a member of the House of Lords, offered to pay Winston one hundred pounds a year towards his expenses. While Winston had some money saved from sales of his books, he decided to use his war fame to make some more. On October 30, 1900, he embarked on a paid speaking tour of Great Britain. He already had a large following through his dispatches from South Africa published in *The Morning Post*. During this tour he used magic lantern slides for the first time. The Boer War appeared to be winding down, and the crowds poured in to hear Winston recount both his escape from the prisoner of war camp in Pretoria and the condition of the people of Ladysmith when it was liberated.

The speaking tour lasted a month, during which time Winston crisscrossed half of Great Britain, speaking once or twice a day and traveling to the next destination on overnight trains. The whirlwind tour left him exhausted, but it had netted him nearly five thousand pounds.

Winston decided to extend his speaking tour to the United States and Canada. When the ship docked in New York City on December 8, Bourke was there to welcome him. That night Winston dined at the Waldorf-Astoria Hotel with Theodore Roosevelt, governor of New York State. Bourke introduced him to many of New York City's influential men. Six days after arriving, Winston gave his first address, at which he was introduced by one of his favorite authors, Mark Twain. It was a heady start to his tour and a wonderful welcome for a man who was half American, half British.

Despite the warm welcome, it didn't take many tour stops for Winston to realize that people in United States had a different attitude towards the Boer War. Americans seemed to have a natural affinity with a nation fighting to maintain its independence from the British Empire. Many people of Dutch descent, including the governor, lived in New York, and they sympathized with the Boers. And in Chicago and other cities with a high population of Irish immigrants, Winston was jeered at as he spoke. It made sense to him; Irish Nationalists wanted their independence from Great Britain and were angry to see the British Empire still grasping to gain more territory.

Winston was relieved when he crossed the border into Canada, part of the British Empire, where he had ten more days of speeches lined up. Much to his relief, he was met with handshakes and cheers everywhere he went.

In Winnipeg, as he was packing to return to England, Winston was puzzled to hear church bells ring out across the city. He soon learned that Queen Victoria had died. It was hard for him to imagine a different monarch. Victoria had been the queen of Great Britain and Ireland since 1837, twelve years before Winston's father's birth. During her reign, the British Empire had grown to encompass 412 million people around the world. Now, the Victorian era was over. Victoria's oldest son would now reign as Edward VII, ushering in the Edwardian era. Winston was eager to get back to London and take up his place in the House of Commons. The arrival of this new era meant new ideas and new opportunities, and he intended to make the most of them.

Back in London, Winston needed somewhere to live. Sunny loaned him a flat in the city that he could use for as long as needed. Winston also decided to try a new form of conveyance—an automobile. He bought a Mors, a car produced by a French manufacturer. He also hired a French chauffeur to keep the vehicle running and drive him around.

By now Jack was back from South Africa and working once more as a stockbroker in London. Winston deposited most of his earnings with Jack's company. The interest on the investment, plus what he continued to earn from book sales, was enough for a single man to live on.

On Thursday, February 14, 1901, Winston Churchill took his seat in the House of Commons. He couldn't help but think of his father, who had walked down the same stairs twenty-six years before on his first day as a conservative member of Parliament.

Although elected as a conservative member of the House of Commons, it wasn't long before Winston realized that he disagreed with his party on many important issues, including military spending, import tariffs, and social reform. As he debated with his fellow politicians, Winston grew more uncomfortable, realizing he had more in common with the Liberal Party than the conservatives.

Tuesday, May 31, 1904, was a decisive day for Winston. That morning he crossed the floor of the House of Commons and sat down beside Liberal leader David Lloyd George. The two men shook hands. Winston was telling the country he was now a liberal. He knew it was a bitter moment for the Conservative Party, which included many powerful men. He would need to watch his back certain that they would seek retribution for his move.

By December 1905, several other conservative members had followed Winston's example and switched allegiance to the Liberal Party. Given the disarray this caused in Parliament, Lord Balfour, the conservative prime minister, resigned. King Edward Vll asked the Liberal Party to form a new government until a general election could be held the following year.

The new liberal prime minister was sixty-nine-year-old Sir Henry Campbell Bannerman. Much to everyone's surprise, Sir Henry appointed Winston to be Undersecretary of the Colonies. Winston could hardly believe his luck. It had, after all, been only a year and a half since he had joined the Liberal Party, and now he held an important post in the government.

The year also ended on a high note for Winston. Four years before, he'd begun work on an ambitious two-volume biography of his father. Now a publisher offered him eight thousand pounds to finish it.

In the general election that followed in early 1906, the Liberal Party won a resounding victory, winning 397 seats in the House of Commons to the Conservatives 156 seats. In the new liberal government, Winston continued in his role as Undersecretary of the Colonies.

In March, following the election, Winston attended a dinner party at Crewe Hall in London, where he was seated next to Clementine Hozier, a tall woman with auburn hair and green-hazel eyes. He remembered seeing her at a ball several years before but had been too intimidated to talk to her. Now he gave her his full attention.

Winston learned that Clementine was the twenty-two-year-old daughter of Lady Blanche Hozier and Sir Henry Hozier, who had died a year ago. Clementine had spent much of her childhood in France and now earned money teaching private French lessons. All of this was fascinating, but what really got Winston's attention was her interest in politics. Clementine was a firm liberal and had well-informed opinions on many issues. When she told him she had spent hours in the gallery at the House of Commons and had seen him debate several times, he was floored. Here was a woman with a grasp on things that really mattered.

Following the dinner party, Winston wanted to see Clementine again, but she had a trip to Germany arranged with her mother. Soon after she left, Jack Churchill announced that he and Lady Gwendeline Bertie were engaged. They had known each other for a long time, but Goonie, as everyone called her, was a Catholic, and her family did not approve of the marriage. Nonetheless, that all seemed to have been worked out, and Jack asked Winston to be his best man. As Winston joined in the wedding preparations, he could see how happy his younger brother was. Perhaps, he wondered, it was time for him to get married as well. At thirty-three years of age, he'd poured all his energy into the military and his political career. He now had a steady income and substantial savings, thanks to his book sales. Yes, he decided, it was indeed time for him to marry, and he had just the woman in mind.

When Clementine returned to London, Winston had his mother invite her to social weekends at her country house. The more time he spent with Clementine, the more Winston was convinced that they were compatible. The couple also wrote interesting letters to each other when apart.

On August 8, 1908, Jack and Goonie were married. A week later Winston invited Clementine to Blenheim Palace where he asked her to marry him. Much to his delight, Clementine said yes. The couple planned to get married a month later.

On the afternoon of September 12, 1908, the bells of nearby Big Ben struck two o'clock as Winston turned to watch Clementine walk down the aisle of St. Margaret's Church, Westminster. Over a thousand guests, including the prime minister, attended the ceremony. Photographers snapped many photos of Winston in his top hat and morning suit and Clementine in her long ivory satin gown and a veil wreathed with orange blossoms. The newspapers dubbed it the "society wedding of the year."

Clementine's aunt hosted a small reception in her home at Portland Place, London. Afterwards, the newly married couple stepped out into a huge crowd who cheered the Undersecretary of the Colonies and his beautiful bride on their way. Winston and Clementine spent the first two nights of their honeymoon at Blenheim Palace as Sunny's guests and then sailed for France, where they caught a train to Italy to stay at Lake Maggiore.

Chapter 11

The Great War

After a six-week honeymoon, Winston and Clementine returned to London and a whirlwind of activity. Winston jumped right back into politics. The Liberal Party was pushing for many social and political reforms, from a minimum wage and maximum working hours for the lower class to increasing taxes on the upper class. The liberals were also confronting the House of Lourds for refusing to ratify the bills sent to them from the House of Commons.

Winston and Clementine leased a house big enough to accommodate them and their four servants. Within a year they hired a fifth servant, a nanny, for their first child, a daughter they named Diana. Around the same time Jack and Goonie had a son, whom they named John. The two couples and their children got along well and visited each other often.

For Winston, 1911 turned out to be a banner year. On May 28, Clementine gave birth to their second child, a son they named Randolph. Five months later Prime Minister Herbert Henry Asquith appointed Winston to serve as First Lord of the Admiralty. Even though it was a time of peace, people, including Winston, were sensing the clouds of war gathering. A web of mutual defense alliances had developed among the various countries of Europe. Under the conditions of these alliances, if one country was attacked by another, those who had a mutual defense alliance with them would come to their aid militarily. Winston saw this network of alliances as similar to a line of dominoes waiting to collapse. Given that the smallest grievance could trigger a massive response, he was determined to do everything possible to update and ready the navy for war. He visited naval stations and dockyards up and down the coast of Great Britain, asking questions and poking around for weaknesses in order to prepare the Royal Navy.

As he went about this job, Winston was particularly interested in how the latest inventions—telephones, telegraphs, automobiles, and airplanes—could help win a war. As he read articles, visited factories, and corresponded with inventors and manufacturers, his mind exploded with possibilities. With field radios, scouts could radio back their observations instead of writing notes to be delivered or setting up a heliograph on a hilltop. Submarines also were becoming an important part of various countries navies.

Winston's attention then turned to naval ships, which used coal as fuel and frequently had to stop at coaling stations to take on more. This was fine in peacetime, but during a war, if a coaling station was bombed or captured, it would have serious consequences. What a disaster it would be for a naval vessel to run out of fuel. Winston thought about the combustion engines now being used in automobiles and motorcycles. Could ships be converted to use them as well? Combustion engines used oil, and a ship could sail much farther before needing to refuel. Winston pushed for all new ships to be built with combustion engines and for older ones to be converted. This led to another problem. Great Britain didn't have its own supply of oil and would have to develop new trading partners to power its navy. This was no easy task, but Winston was able to convince Parliament to buy the rights to oil fields in Persia.

And then there was Winston's favorite new invention—airplanes, which had fascinated him ever since the time the Wright brothers first flew one in the United States eight years before. He was even more excited when French aviator Louis Bleriot designed an airplane and flew from England and France for the first time in 1909.

Winston could see a thousand potential uses for airplanes in modern warfare. They could fly over enemy lines, shoot down at soldiers from above, drop bombs, even parachute men and supplies into enemy territory. And how, if there was a way to combine airplanes and radios or photography, would that change things? Winston knew he had to learn to fly so he could understand this new technology for himself. It was a dangerous pursuit, and

Clementine tried to stop him, but Winston loved the exhilarating experience of being up in the sky and able to move in three dimensions. Soon he heard of another astonishing invention: airplanes that could take off and land on water. Winston started calling them seaplanes. He asked Parliament to give him funds to build one hundred of them at a time when no one else in the House of Commons knew that such a thing even existed.

All this information gathering was great fun for Winston, but he never lost sight of his goal. There were constant reminders that Europe was unstable. Germany passed a law to drastically increase the size of the German navy to equal that of Great Britain's. Winston viewed this with alarm and vowed to build two British battleships for every new one that Germany built. At the same time, however, he urged Germany and Great Britain to jointly commit to building fewer battleships. Germany's leader Kaiser Wilhelm II refused to cooperate, which made Winston surer than ever that Germany and Great Britain were on a collision path.

During this time, Winston also had a family challenge to deal with. His mother confided that her husband George Cornwallis-West, had left her for a famous actress. The split hadn't yet become public knowledge but it soon would be known that George wanted a divorce so he could be free to remarry. Jennie Churchill's marriage had caused a scandal in 1900, and another scandal was inevitable now that it was ending. Winston did what he could to help his mother through the difficult situation.

At the same time, Clementine announced that their third child was due in October. As relations with Germany deteriorated further, Winston was greatly concerned about the kind of world the new baby might be born into.

On June 28, 1914, Winston was working at home when he received a telegram informing him that Archduke Franz Ferdinand and his wife had been assassinated. The archduke was heir to the Austro-Hungarian throne and was shot to death while visiting Sarajevo, capital of Bosnia-Herzegovina. Winston's heart lurched at the news. Was this the match that would ignite a war? He soon learned more details. The shooter was a young Serb avenging the Austro-Hungarian annexation of his country in 1908. The Austro-Hungarians demanded that Serbia pay an enormous sum of money to them as compensation for the assassination.

A month later, on Tuesday, July 28, when the Serbs refused to pay, the Austro-Hungarian Empire declared war on Serbia. And then the dominoes began to fall just as Winston feared they would. Russia had a mutual defense alliance with Serbia and came to its aid, and then Germany declared war on Russia. Germany asked France to stay out of the conflict, but France already had a mutual defense alliance with Russia. The French had promised that if Germany or Austria-Hungary attacked Russia, France would aid them with a million French troops. France joined the conflict on Russia's side. Germany declared war on France, and the French declared war on Germany. The Germans then invaded Belgium to get to France. But Great Britain had an alliance with Belgium. France declared war on Austria-Hungary, while the Austro-Hungarians declared war on Russia and Serbia declared war on Germany. Then Italy sided with France and Great Britain.

On Monday, August 3, 1914, as the mutual alliance dominoes fell across Europe, Prime Minister Asquith sent an ultimatum to Germany. He demanded that the Germans stop their invasion of Belgium by 11:00 p.m. or the British would declare war on them. Winston paced the floor of the Admiralty office that night, monitoring incoming phone calls and telegrams. At 11:00 p.m. he heard Big Ben toll. There had been no word from the Germans, who had ignored the ultimatum. Great Britain was now at war with Germany. Winston ordered an urgent message be sent to the British navy and military facilities around the world. The message read, "Commence hostilities against Germany." Then he heard music. Thousands of people had gathered outside Buckingham Palace to sing "God Save the King."

With the country now at war, Winston phoned Clementine, who was away on holiday at the beach. Her mother was living in Paris, and arrangements needed to be made to get her safely back to England as quickly as possible. The next day, Jack phoned to say he was off to join the Oxfordshire Yeomanry, where he'd maintained a position as a reserve officer.

As First Lord of the Admiralty, Winston spent his hours planning for war. His immediate concerns were how to transport troops to the fighting in France, blockade Germany, stop the German navy from leaving the Baltic and North Sea, and keep British trade routes with its empire open. Keeping the shipping routes open was particularly important, since Great Britain and Germany were the only countries in the war that did not produce enough food to feed themselves. If ships were blocked from entering port for long enough, the British people would starve.

Germany and her allies, known as the Central Powers, were engaged in fighting on two fronts—in the east against Russia and in the west in France. By October 1914, the war on the Western Front in France had bogged down. Just as Winston had predicted, rapid fire machine guns had revolutionized warfare. The old standard practice of marching line after line of troops into battle against machine guns was suicide. Instead, troops on both sides dug into long, muddy trenches, from which they fired potshots at each other. Before long the trenches stretched for 475 miles, from the English Channel to the Swiss Alps.

At the same time, the German army continued its push into Belgium, taking control of more of the country. At the beginning of October 1914, the city of Antwerp was about to fall to the Germans. Faced with this, Winston got permission from Parliament to send three thousand men to help defend the city. He flew to Antwerp on October 3 to lead them. The soldiers were unable to save the city from falling into enemy hands, but they held the Germans at bay for a week. In that time the Belgian army was able to escape and make its way to ports along the English Channel to be shipped to England.

Before the Germans overran Antwerp, Winston was able to escape and make it safely back to England. When he got home a new baby was waiting for him—a daughter, whom Clementine had named Sarah during Winston's absence.

On October 29, 1914, the Ottoman Empire launched a surprise attack against Russian ports on the Black Sea. The raid was carried out with the knowledge and support of Germany. As a result, on November 1 Russia declared war on the Ottomans. In response, on November 5 Great Britain and France, Russia's allies also declared war on the Ottoman Empire.

In December 1914, the German navy began bombarding the British ports of Scarborough, Hartlepool, and Whitby. These attacks resulted in 137 deaths and 592 people wounded, many of them civilians. The population of Great Britain was shocked. The war was no longer a war "over there on the Continent." It had now reached into the people's own towns and villages. The British population mobilized as never before. Everyone looked around for some way to help. Five-year-old children scoured city dumps, looking for scrap metal that could be used for making guns. Even though the age for leaving school was officially twelve years old, boys as young as ten lined up to work in airplane factories. Boy Scouts guarded railway tunnels while Girl Guides ripped sheets into bandages. Secretaries practiced carrying stretchers through city streets, housewives dug up parks and grew potatoes, and old men knotted rope to make camouflage nets.

Winston's family joined in the effort along with everyone else. His mother played the piano for a famous singer who gave free concerts for soldiers, and his sister-in-law Goonie went to work at All Saints Hospital, serving on a ward for seriously wounded officers. Clementine volunteered with the Young Women's Christian Association (YWCA), where she supervised the opening, staffing, and running of canteens that fed five hundred women working in munitions factories.

Given everything going on around him, Winston knew that he had to find a way to relax. He needed something that would keep him from buckling under the incredible pressure he faced. He took up oil painting. Whenever he needed to clear his head, he would set up his easel and paints in a tranquil spot in the countryside and get lost for an hour or two in the beauty of nature.

In January 1915, with the Western Front at a stalemate, Grand Duke Nicholas, commander of the Russian armies, asked the British government to attack Turkey. He hoped this would relieve the pressure Russian troops were experiencing fighting the Ottomans in the Caucasus region. Winston thought over the request and decided the most strategic place to attack would be the Dardanelles, a thirty-eight-mile-long channel that led to Constantinople. If the British navy could force its way up the channel and occupy the city, it would provide the relief the Russians were seeking. The Dardanelles campaign began in mid-February 1915.

By mid-March three British battleships had been sunk and three more damaged. Winston knew this could not go on. The Admiralty had to come up with a new plan. Rather than force their way up the channel to Constantinople, a land force would come ashore at two places on the Gallipoli Peninsula, capture it, and then turn their attention to the Dardanelles channel on the other side of the peninsula.

At the end of April, British troops landed at Cape Helles, while the Australian and New Zealand Army Corps (ANZAC) landed on the narrow beaches farther up the peninsula.

Winston waited anxiously to see how the attack played out. He knew that war strategies were a gamble, but he was a gambler. There was only a thin strip of sandy beach where the Australian and New Zealand troops came ashore, behind which rose steep cliffs. It was soon apparent that the ANZACs who waded ashore had no chance against the Turks and their machine guns embedded above. They mowed down the invaders by the thousands as they came ashore and tried to scale the cliff face. The operation was a disaster. By the time it was over, conservative members of Parliament were asking tough questions about who was making the decisions and how they were being made.

In the face of this opposition, Prime Minister Asquith was forced to ask the liberals to form a coalition government with the conservatives. It only seemed fair that both parties should have a say in the vital decisions being made that impacted every man, woman, and child in Great Britain, along with millions more across the empire. However, one of the conservative demands for joining such a government was that Winston Churchill be fired as First Lord of the Admiralty. He had turned his back on the conservatives back in 1904 and crossed the floor of the House of Commons to join the liberals, and now it seemed it was payback time from his old party. They wanted nothing to do with him. In truth, many Liberal Party members also wanted Winston sidelined after the failure at Gallipoli. And so, Winston Churchill was stripped of his title and position at the Admiralty and demoted to the lowly cabinet position of Chancellor of the Duchy of Lancaster. It was a bitter blow for a man of action. Winston desperately wanted to be doing something useful, something that contributed to the war effort. But what?

By November 1915, Winston couldn't stand aside any longer. If he couldn't serve his country in Parliament, he would fight on the battlefield. He resigned his cabinet post and hurried to the Western Front as a lieutenant colonel in the 6th Royal Scots Fusiliers. Clementine protested, but Winston knew he had to do something. The Fusiliers were embedded in the trenches along the Belgian Front near Ploegsteert. At first the soldiers under his command didn't welcome Winston. They were skeptical that a member of Parliament would be of much practical use to them. But Winston soon won them over. He was willing to be knee deep in mud in the trenches and made sure to take his turn doing daily duties. When their trench was under fire, Winston was right there with his men, risking death with them from snipers or artillery shells. Bullets came within inches of hitting him, but he proved himself to be as brave and competent as the best of his men.

In mid-May 1916, the army on the Western Front was rearranged, and the 6th Royal Scots Fusiliers were merged with another division. Winston had led them for six months and proven himself effective on the front lines, but now he had to decide whether to stay with this new division or do something else. He decided to return to England, hoping everyone had moved on from the Gallipoli debacle and he would be able to help shape war policy again. That did not happen. When Winston returned to the House of Commons, his frustration grew when no one seemed interested in his thoughts on long-range strategies to win the war.

Parliament was rife with factions, and in October 1916 Herbert Asquith resigned as prime minster. He was succeeded by David Lloyd George, which gave Winston new hope. He liked the new prime minister and felt he had a better chance of returning to the inner circle directing the war effort. This did not happen immediately, but eight months later, David Lloyd George appointed him Minister of Munitions. Now Winston was back in the thick of things. He was soon out and about visiting munitions factories, encouraging the women workers manning them, and suggesting ways to improve production.

By April 1917, German U–boats had attacked and sunk many U.S. merchant ships delivering food and munitions to Great Britain, even though the United States and Germany were not at war with each other. Americans were incensed at the loss of lives, ships, and cargo. They were being pulled into the war whether they wanted it or not. It was time to act. On April 4, 1917, the United States Senate passed a declaration of war on Germany, followed two days later by an affirmative vote in the House of Representatives. President Wilson then formally declared the country to be at war. Great Britain now had a powerful new ally, bringing more men and equipment on their way.

As had been predicted, the influx of thousands of troops and military equipment from the United States turned the tide of war in the Allies' favor. At first the Germans tried to stiffen their resistance, but first their supplies and then their resolve ran low. On November 11, 1918, the Great War that had engulfed Europe for more than four years ended.

Across Great Britain church bells rang out. People thronged into the streets cheering, dancing, and throwing confetti. The war was over! They had survived. The soldiers were coming home.

Chapter 12

Chancellor of the Exchequer

Four days after the war ended, on November 15, 1918, Winston and Clementine welcomed another baby daughter. They gave her the most cheerful name they could think of—Marigold. Their daughter Sarah had been born at the beginning of the war. Marigold's birth heralded a fresh start. Winston hoped she would grow up and live in a time of peace and prosperity.

While the war had ended, Parliament and the cabinet were kept busy. An armistice had been signed ending the fighting on the battlefield, but now the Allies needed to draw up a final treaty officially ending the Great War. It would also determine how the defeated Central Powers should be treated. The treaty was negotiated at the Paris Peace Conference that started on January 18, 1919, with many leaders from Allied countries taking part. Most of the major discussions and decisions made were guided by the leaders of the "Big Four" Allied nations: Prime Minister David Lloyd George of Great Britain, Prime Minister Georges Clemenceau of France, President Woodrow Wilson of the United States, and Prime Minister Vittorio Orlando of Italy. By the end of the process, the German Empire, the Russian Empire, the Ottoman Empire, and the Austro-Hungarian Empire were all gone. Several new independent countries emerged, including Poland, Finland, Yugoslavia, and Czechoslovakia. Germany was also forced to disarm and pay 132 billion marks in reparations for the loss and damage they had caused in Europe, and their previous provinces of Alsace-Lorraine were given to France. Germany's overseas territories were taken away and redistributed to other countries.

Not only was the map of the world redrawn in the years after the end of the Great War, but also Great Britain became a different place. Over 700,000 British soldiers lay dead in foreign graves. Two million more returned home maimed and shell-shocked. The euphoria of winning the war soon wore off. Many of the returning soldiers were unemployable because of their physical or psychological injuries. Great Britain faced massive social problems.

Winston understood how difficult it was to adjust to this new normal. He had lost five cousins and an uncle to the fighting in the war, along with numerous soldier friends he had fought alongside during his time spent in the British army.

Other causes of social unrest also became evident. Many women had found a new freedom as they stepped into jobs men had traditionally held. They enjoyed the freedom of earning their own money. They protested for the right to vote and won some concessions. Women in Great Britain who were over thirty years of age who were householders or owned their own property were given the vote, along with all men over the age of twenty-one, regardless of whether they owned property or not. Both men and women wanted other rights for themselves and their children—the right to a good education, to free health care, and to band together in the workplace and form trade unions. Everyone seemed to have an opinion about what should change in Britain.

Parliament kept busy trying to juggle these new expectations. In 1921 Winston was appointed to a new Cabinet position. He became Secretary of State for the Colonies, a powerful role overseeing the administration of Great Britain's colonies. Although four European empires had collapsed because of the war, the British Empire, though it was forever changed, had survived.

In his new position, Winston helped guide and evolve the way that Great Britain would manage and oversee its colonies. He also played a key role in negotiating the Anglo-Irish Treaty. The year before, Parliament had partitioned Ireland into two self-governing territories within the United Kingdom: Northern Ireland, which encompassed the six northeastern counties on the island that were predominantly Protestant; and the Irish Free State, comprising the remaining predominantly Catholic counties in the south. Both territories had their own elected Parliament. The Anglo-Irish Treaty, which Winston helped negotiate, provided for the establishment of the Irish Free State as a self-governing dominion within the British Empire. This would give it the same self-governing status as Canada, Australia, and New Zealand.

As he worked away at the situation in Ireland, Winston received some sad news. On April 19, 1921, Clementine's only brother, Bill Hozier, had killed himself in a hotel room in Paris. He had been a destroyer commander in the navy during the war, and his death came as a bitter blow. It reminded Winston that thousands of men who had fought in the war bore terrible mental scars as a result.

Five weeks after Bill's death, Winston's mother slipped on some stairs and broke her ankle. Winston rushed to her bedside at the hospital where she had surgery to reset the ankle. The operation went well, but soon gangrene set in. A week later a surgeon had to amputate Jennie's leg above the knee. Winston worried about how she would adjust to spending the rest of her life in a wheelchair. But it wasn't to be. On June 29, 1921, an artery in her leg burst, and she bled to death within minutes. Winston could hardly believe it. His sixty-seven-year-old mother, once so full of fun and energy, was dead. Winston struggled to deal with his loss. But worse was yet to come.

Less than eight weeks later, the four Churchill children were staying at the beach in Kent with their new nanny. Clementine was visiting friends in Cheshire while Winston worked in London. Unbeknownst to either of them, Marigold had become ill. It started with a cough and a low temperature, which the new nanny thought she could deal with herself. But when Marigold's temperature soared, Clementine and Winston were informed, and they both rushed to be with their daughter. Winston called in the best doctors, but it was too late. What had started as a simple throat infection had quickly spread throughout Marigold's body. She died two days later, Winston and Clementine at her side. Tuesday, August 23,1921, was the darkest day of their lives.

Winston did his best to put the awful summer of 1921 behind him. A year later, Clementine gave birth to another daughter, whom they named Mary. And while she did not take Marigold's place, she did drive away the silence that had befallen the Churchills' nursery.

Soon after Mary's birth, Winston thought deeply about providing a real home for his family. They had lived in many places over the years, including the Admiralty House, and with Jack and Goonie and with Winston's mother. Winston now longed for a place where his children could have stability and freedom.

Winston visited many country houses looking for the perfect one. And then he found Chartwell, a large, two-story redbrick country home in the Kent countryside, twenty-five miles southeast of London. He smiled as he rode a horse around the perimeter of the property. Many years ago, his nanny, Mrs. Everest, had told him that Kent was the most beautiful county in England. As he rode across it, Winston had to agree with her. He loved the sweeping view across the Kentish Weald, and his imagination ran wild with possibilities. He would engineer terraces and ponds, construct an outdoor swimming pool with floodlights and heating, even build an elaborate tree house for the younger children.

Clementine, though, was not enthusiastic about the place. She pointed out to Winston that the house was dilapidated and in need of a major remodel to make it fit for a family to inhabit. Winston agreed, but his love for the grounds and surrounding countryside propelled him forward. By the end of 1922 Chartwell belonged to him. But before the family could move into their new home, Winston rented a house nearby for them to live in while an architect and tradesmen worked to repair and remodel the old brick buildings. He didn't hire a landscaper. He wanted to the grounds work himself.

A month later Winston had to undergo emergency surgery to have his appendix removed. It was an election year, and post-surgery Winston was too weak to campaign effectively for reelection. Clementine, baby Mary in tow, did her best to rally support for her husband, but it wasn't enough. Winston lost his reelection bid. "In the twinkling of an eye, I found myself without an office, without a seat, without a party, and without an appendix," he joked.

Although he hated to be out of the hustle and bustle of politics Winston had plenty of other things to fill his time. He began writing *The World Crisis*, a six-volume series of books that would cover many aspects of the Great War.

It took three years for the architect and tradesmen to complete the repairs and build a new east wing onto the house. In April 1924 the Churchill family officially moved into Chartwell. By now fourteen-year-old Diana and twelve-year-old Randolph were attending boarding school. Meanwhile, nine-year-old Sarah attended the local school while two-and-a-half-year-old Mary was looked after by her nanny. Winston was delighted that Diana and Sarah shared his love of animals. Together they turned Chartwell into a menagerie. They owned ponies and parrots, cats, dogs, chickens, black swans, even golden orfes. It was just what Winston had imagined for his growing family.

Between writing sessions, Winston worked on Chartwell's grounds. He dammed a spring to create three lakes, where the golden orfes swam. He learned how to lay bricks and rebuilt many of the stone walls around Chartwell. He also set up his own art studio.

Meanwhile, British politics were undergoing some swift changes. Winston hardly recognized the Liberal Party. He felt more aligned with the Conservative Party, particularly on how important it was to develop free trade with other countries. At the end of October 1924, six months after moving into Chartwell, Winston campaigned once more for a seat in the House of Commons, this time as a conservative. The conservatives swept into power in the election, taking Winston along with them. He became the member of Parliament for Epping, in Essex.

The new prime minster, Stanley Baldwin, named Winston to be Chancellor of the Exchequer. It was an unexpected honor for Winston, who was about to celebrate his fiftieth birthday. Many people protested that it was the second most powerful role after prime minister, and they didn't think it should go to someone who'd just changed parties. Winston appreciated the trust Stanley Baldwin had placed in him. He wished his mother was alive to see it. Thirty-eight years ago his father had been given the same position. For the next four and a half years, between November 1924 and May 1929, Winston worked hard fulfilling the role of Chancellor of the Exchequer. Great Britain continued to be roiled by tremendous social problems and faced many difficult challenges.

By 1929, the people of Great Britain wanted change, and in the parliamentary election in May that year the Conservatives lost to the Labour Party, which had all but replaced the old Liberal Party and had won in a landslide. Once again Winston lost his ministerial role in government, though he was reelected to represent the Epping electorate.

Following the election, fifty-five-year-old Winston retreated to Chartwell. There were still landscaping projects to do there, books to write, speeches to give, friends to entertain, scenes to paint. There was no doubt he had plenty to occupy himself with.

One of the first activities Winston decided to undertake was a three-month speaking tour of Canada and the United States. Nearly thirty years had passed since his previous visit to both countries. He invited Jack and their sons Johnny and Randolph along. The party traveled in luxury. The Canadian Pacific Railway Company gifted them several railcars and servants for the twenty-four hundred-mile trip from Quebec in the east to Vancouver on the West Coast. Whenever Winston was scheduled to stop and give a lecture along the way, their railcars were detached from the train and shunted onto a siding. When they were ready to move on, their railcars would be coupled to the next train heading west, and off they went again.

After a month traveling through Canada, the group crossed the border into the United States. They stayed with the American politician and newspaper publisher William Randolph Hearst, who arranged a star-studded night for Winston at a mansion in Santa Monica, California. There Winston was introduced to the famous British-born actor Charlie Chaplin, and the two talked until three in the morning about their mutual love of military history.

The head of Bethlehem Steel provided a special train to take the touring party from California back to the East Coast. There Johnny and Randolph boarded a ship to return to Great Britain and their university studies. Winston and Jack stayed on in the United States to visit several famous Civil War sites.

Winston and Jack were in New York City on Thursday, October 24, 1929, when an event took place there that would rock the world—the Wall Street Crash. On that day, which was soon being called Black Thursday, the New York Stock Exchange experienced the largest sell-off of shares in U.S. history. In less than a week the collapse of the stock market meant that investors had lost around 25 billion dollars. The collapse reverberated around the world, creating even deeper losses for investors. Jack, who managed Winston's investments, informed his brother that a good portion of his money had been lost in the crash, including the money he'd earned on the tour. Winston returned home to Chartwell a poorer man. For him it was more important than ever to bring in money from his writing projects. He started writing a book about his ancestor John Churchill, the first duke of Marlborough.

In 1932, Winston visited Germany to view battlefields where his ancestor had led the British to victory. But what he saw in Germany alarmed him. The peace treaty Germany had signed to end the war expressly forbade the country from rearming its military as well as paying reparations for the damage it had caused in the war. However, a new voice had arisen in Germany, that of the National Socialist German Workers Party (Nazis) led by a short, fiery Austrian named Adolf Hitler. Hitler and the Nazis questioned why Germany should have to honor those commitments. They were rearming at an alarming speed. Who had the energy and the resources to stop them?

Back in England, Winston did everything he could to alert his fellow countrymen to what he saw as the rising threat in Germany. But no one wanted to hear it. Following the Wall Street Crash, the world had fallen into the Great Depression. All eyes in Great Britain were focused on the economic problems the country faced, not on the rise of a Fascist political party half a continent away in Germany.

On December 12, 1932, Diana Churchill married John Bailey, son of Sir Abraham Bailey who had amassed millions of pounds from mining contracts in South Africa. The couple were married at St. Margaret's Church, Westminster, the same church in which Winston and Clementine had married twenty-four years before.

Meanwhile Germany had held a federal election in November 1932. The Communist Party made big gains in the election, but no one party won a majority of the votes. However, the Nazi Party's vote share was the highest, enough for the party to form a coalition government. As a result, on January 30, 1933, six weeks after Diana and John's wedding, Adolf Hitler was sworn in as chancellor of Germany to head the new government. A month later, on February 27,1933, a mysterious fire burned down the Reichstag, the German Parliament building. Adolf Hitler immediately blamed the fire on Communist agitators and persuaded the German Parliament to pass an Enabling Act. Once passed, this act gave Hitler complete power over the lives of the German people. There would be no more elections, no more high court appeals, no more justice. Adolf Hitler was now the sole leader of Germany—the Führer.

Winston followed the events closely. He was sickened as Hitler and the Nazis abolished trade unions, banned all other political parties and gleefully sent 150,000 key political and trade union leaders and supporters off to concentration camps.

Members of the British Parliament, aware that these things were happening, were unwilling to entertain the possibility that Germany would start another European war. It was too painful for them to contemplate such death and destruction happening again. After all, they countered, wasn't the Great War supposed to be the war to end all wars? Members of Parliament and Cabinet ministers preferred to talk of peace, of pacifying Germany, of looking the other way when it broke its treaties. Surely, they argued, Germany, wouldn't go too far. It didn't want more carnage either. Winston disagreed with their position and their reasoning. While others turned aside, he looked war in the eye. He knew in his bones that it was coming and that he had to rouse the British people to make the sacrifices necessary to face it head on.

Chapter 13

Peace For Our Time or Not?

For the next five years, Winston continued to represent Epping in the House of Commons. Although the conservatives were back in power, he held no Cabinet position and was relegated to the back benches of Parliament. Throughout this time Winston grew more alarmed at how Hitler and the Nazis manipulated the German people, and he did what he could to direct people's attention to the mounting threat.

Because few politicians paid attention to his warnings, Winston appealed to the British public. He wrote hundreds of articles for magazines and newspapers and gave speeches and radio addresses. He was constantly accused of being a war monger, of stirring up conflict. But Winston didn't want war. He wanted to push Great Britain to build up its military strength to deter Hitler's army from attacking anyone.

But Hitler would not be stopped. On March 11, 1938, German troops marched into Austria. The Austrians sent an urgent message to Great Britain asking for help, but the British Parliament was unwilling to act quickly. In response, Winston gave a stirring speech in the House of Commons warning lawmakers they could not underestimate Hitler. This was just the beginning, and a swift response was called for. But Prime Minster Neville Chamberlain preached appeasement, giving in to Hitler's demands in the hope he would be satisfied taking Austria and stop there. Winston, on the other hand, argued that Hitler would never be satisfied until he ruled Europe.

In early September, the British government learned that Germany was preparing to invade the Sudetenland in Czechoslovakia, where three million ethnic Germans lived. Winston visited the prime minister at 10 Downing Street and begged him to tell the Germans that Great Britain would declare war on them if they invaded Czechoslovakia. Instead, the prime minister declared that he would travel to Germany himself to persuade Hitler to stop the planned invasion. Winston left 10 Downing Street with a sense of doom. He was doing all that he could do. Why couldn't others see the growing danger in Europe?

On September 30, 1938, Neville Chamberlain met with Adolf Hitler in Germany. The two leaders smiled, shook hands, negotiated, and signed the

Munich Agreement. This allowed Germany to take control of Sudetenland in exchange for promising not to invade any other countries.

The jubilant prime minister returned to Great Britain and went straight to Buckingham Palace, where he was congratulated by King George VI. Neville Chamberlain was then driven to 10 Downing Street where five thousand people had gathered to give him a hero's welcome home. He waved the agreement that he and Adolf Hitler had signed and declared, "My good friends, I believe it is peace for our time. We thank you from the bottom of our hearts. Now I recommend you go home and sleep quietly in your beds." But Winston couldn't sleep quietly. He was certain that Hitler had no intention of abiding by the Munich Agreement. As far as he was concerned, Chamberlain had been duped and Great Britain was in grave danger.

Sure enough, in March 1939, six months after the signing of the Munich Agreement, Germany invaded the rest of Czechoslovakia. Then on September 1, 1939, the German army marched into Poland. Other European countries scrambled to defend themselves. The government of Great Britain, believing Hitler would bomb its industrial cities, activated Operation Pied Piper. This entailed loading up one and a half million vulnerable people living in the cities, including eight hundred thousand children, and relocating them to the countryside.

Meanwhile on September 3, Chamberlain finally admitted he'd misread Adolf Hitler. He had been a fool. Appeasement had failed. At 11:15 a.m. Great

Britain declared war on Germany. The lives of millions of people—soldiers and civilians—were about to be upended.

Within hours of declaring war, Chamberlain asked Winston to again take up the role of First Lord of the Admiralty. Despite being sixty-five years old, Winston relished the challenge. He knew it would be more daunting than anything he'd faced before, but he was back at the Admiralty and ready for action. During his previous stint in the role, Winston had championed new, modern technologies that were incorporated into the armed forces. Now the new technology would play an increased and important role in the war. This was particularly true of tanks and airplanes. Tanks were now more mobile and better armed and were an important part of armies around the world. And by 1939, airplanes bore almost no resemblance to the ones used in the Great War. During that war they were flimsy and flew so low they were often shot down with rifle fire from the ground. That seemed so old-fashioned. Airplanes were now bigger, more powerful, and better armed. Bombers could drop massive loads of bombs on a target from high above.

The British Expeditionary Force was immediately dispatched to help the French defend against any German attacks. Airplanes from the Royal Air Force (RAF) were also deployed to France. And as quickly as they could be assembled, more British fighting units, this time men of the Territorial Army were able to cross the English Channel. Within weeks Great Britain had sent over 200,000 men to France.

For the next eight months, British forces and their European allies slowed Germany's advance but were unable to stop it. The Germans occupied neutral Norway in April 1940, and then on May 10, German forces crossed into The Netherlands, also a neutral country. When Prime Minister Chamberlain was informed that Hitler had indeed invaded The Netherlands, he finally bowed to public pressure and resigned his position. Within hours, Winston was summoned to Buckingham Palace, where King George VI asked him to lead a new government. As he was driven back to Admiralty House in his limousine, Winston was sobered. He was now the tip of the spear—the man who would lead his country into battle against a ruthless dictator and his powerful army. The day he had predicted for so long had arrived. Winston turned to his bodyguard and said, "I hope that it is not too late. I am very much afraid that it is. We can only do our best."

Winston spent the weekend writing a speech to be delivered on Monday. His aim was to prepare Parliament and the nation for the long, difficult task ahead. On Monday he declared to members of Parliament, "I have nothing to offer but blood, toil, tears and sweat... You can ask, what is our policy? I can answer in one word: It is victory, victory at all cost, victory in spite of all terror, victory, however long and hard the road may be; for without victory, there is no survival."

The following day, May 14, 1940, Winston learned that The Netherlands had fallen to the Nazis. Now the Germans were advancing into Belgium and

France. The Dutch Queen Wilhelmina and her family fled to London as 230,000 British Expeditionary Forces and 70,000 French troops were being pushed back by the Germans. That evening French Prime Minister Paul Reynaud called Winston to inform him that over half the British Air Force planes in France had been destroyed. He pleaded for more airplanes.

Winston wondered if the French prime minister was exaggerating. Surely France, one of the three strongest military forces in the world, wouldn't fall so quickly—they must have more men, more weapons, more determination than that. Winston knew he needed to see the situation on the ground for himself. Less than a week after becoming prime minister, Winston boarded an RAF de Havilland D.H. 95 Flamingo airplane at Hendon Aerodrome in London. The aircraft was escorted by fighter planes as Winston flew to Paris to speak with Paul Reynaud.

Winston soon found out it was true. The French leaders were unwilling to fight to the last man. They had accepted defeat and were looking for ways to live alongside the Nazis. Winston was disgusted. In his speech he had urged the British people never to surrender. Why weren't the French leaders doing the same?

When he returned to London, Winston wrote to President Franklin Roosevelt to warn him that if the United States waited too long to join Great Britain in the war, it may be too late for them all. In the past ten days the British navy had lost eleven destroyers to German attacks. Winston asked the president to loan Great Britain fifty mothballed destroyers from the Great War and to sell them new airplanes and ammunition. President Roosevelt responded by exchanging the fifty destroyers for ninety-nine-year leases on British bases in the Caribbean and Newfoundland. Winston was grateful. He knew that the president was taking a political risk helping Great Britain. Most Americans wanted their country to stay out of another war in Europe.

Meanwhile, the French army and British and Belgian troops were being driven back towards the northern coast of France. By May 25, 1940, the situation was dire. Three hundred thirty-eight thousand British, Belgian, and French soldiers were trapped on the beaches and harbor of Dunkirk. If these soldiers were captured or killed, the war would be over. Their fate hung in the balance. Winston had to evacuate them. Ships were the only option, although the beaches around Dunkirk were shallow and large ships would have to anchor offshore while the men were ferried to them. But how could they get the men from the shore to the ships? Winston ordered any shallow draft seaworthy boats, large or small, that could be used to ferry troops from shore to navy ships to head across the English Channel to Dunkirk. Eight hundred vessels, from river barges to fishing boats, crewed by factory workers, farmers, retirees, and hobbyist sailors were soon on their way to rescue the troops. The weather, which could be unpredictable in May, was perfect for the operation.

Close to 340,000 (including 123,000 French soldiers) were successfully evacuated. Publicly, Winston called this a miracle, but privately he understood the true cost of the operation. Over twenty-six thousand French soldiers had been evacuated on the last day, but thirty thousand to forty thousand more had to be left behind and captured by the Germans. Around seventeen thousand troops died during the evacuation. The British army also had to leave seven hundred tanks, eight hundred and eighty heavy artillery pieces, eleven thousand machine guns, and sixty-four thousand vehicles behind. This equipment was not only Britain's loss but also Hitler's gain. Two hundred and fifty Royal Air Force fighter planes and their pilots had been shot down in just ten days, and now they had fewer than five hundred fighter planes left. The prospect of Great Britain standing alone for much longer against the Germans looked grim.

Now that much of France was being overrun by the Germans, Winston knew that he needed to speak to the House of Commons about the path ahead. In his speech he declared, "We shall defend our island, whatever the cost may be. We shall fight on the beaches, we shall fight on the landing grounds, we shall fight in the fields and in the streets, we shall fight in the hills; we shall never surrender."

Less than a week later, on June 10, Winston received more bad news. Benito Mussolini, Italy's Fascist dictator, formally joined ranks with Adolf Hitler and declared war on France and Great Britain. Winston made four more daring flights to those parts of France the Germans had not yet conquered, attempting to strengthen French resolve. On June 14, 1940, the German army marched into Paris.

When he learned this, Winston swung into action once more. He flew to Bordeaux, where the French leadership had now retreated. After meeting with them, it was obvious that the French government was going to capitulate to German demands. Winston urged the leaders to order the ships of the mighty French fleet to sail to England where they could join with the British navy instead of falling into the hands of the Germans. They refused, and on June 17, Paul Reynaud resigned as France's prime minister. He was replaced by Marshal Philippe Pétain, an eighty-four-year-old French hero of the Great War. Five days later, Pétain commanded the French army to lay down its arms and surrender. The Germans and Italians were now in control of almost all Western Europe.

Winston was appalled. When the war began, he never imagined that France, with its magnificent army and navy, would give up so easily. Now he needed to assure the British public that their government would never do the same, that they would fight to the last man. In a speech Winston admonished his fellow countrymen, "Let us therefore brace ourselves to our duty and so bear ourselves that if the British Empire and its Commonwealth lasts for a thousand years men will still say, 'This was their finest hour.'" The speech had a calming effect on the nation. Winston's call to have courage fortified British resolve to resist no matter what Adolf Hitler and his army did. Winston realized that his words were as powerful as any bullets.

Privately, Winston felt that Great Britain couldn't win the war without the United States joining them.

He wrote and talked on the telephone regularly with President Roosevelt, but he got mixed messages. The president privately urged Winston to stand firm, that the United States stood with the British. Yet publicly he insisted he was bound by the Neutrality Act of 1937 that banned the shipment or sale of arms from the United States to any nation at war.

Now that most of France was occupied, the German air force, the Luftwaffe, gained a tremendous advantage. It was able to use airfields along France's northern coast and be flying over Great Britain six minutes later. Day after day, it targeted industrial and military sites in Britain. People living in southern England grew used to British and German fighters engaging in fierce dog fights. Fighter planes crashed into the wheat fields of Kent and school yards in Dover. Home guardsmen arrested German pilots who escaped the crashes and marched them to local police stations.

On Saturday, September 7, 1940, Winston was in the Cabinet War Rooms complex, located beneath the massive Treasury building in Whitehall, London. He was told British radar had detected a massive number of German airplanes headed directly for London. He had been expecting this to happen. Runners brought Winston more details. About three hundred and fifty German bombers and six hundred fighter planes formed a grid in the air twenty miles wide and forty miles long. Everyone braced himself. A few minutes later, people felt the walls vibrate. London was being pummeled from above. Winston hurried between the map room and the radar room, monitoring the positions of the bombers as well as the RAF aircraft trying to shoot them out of the sky. Twelve hours passed before an eerie silence fell over London. The bombing had stopped.

When dawn broke, Winston visited the East End, which had been hit hard. He got out of his car and walked among the wreckage. The stench of gunpowder filled his nostrils and sulphur stung his eyes as he witnessed dead bodies carried from demolished houses and buildings. Union Jack flags—some made of cloth, others handmade with paper and crayons—flew atop piles of rubble. Winston reached for a handkerchief to wipe the tears that spilled down his face. Then he waved his hand high and made a *V* sign with his fingers—V for victory. He had to make the British public believe that if they just kept going through the carnage, they would be victorious.

On the return drive to the War Rooms, Winston thought back to the conversation he had forty-nine years before at Harrow when he told Murland Evans about his dream of the future. "I shall be in command of the defense of London, and I shall save it and England from disaster," he remembered saying. And now, extraordinary as it seemed, he was doing exactly that.

Later that night, the whine of German airplanes was heard once more over London. Sirens blared as men, women, and children sprinted for the nearest bomb shelter. Winston's staff and Clementine urged him to retreat to the bunker in the basement of 10 Downing Street, but Winston refused to go. He couldn't hide. This time he needed to experience it for himself.

Morning after morning Winston went out with teams of volunteers to assess the damage from the overnight bombing. Thousands of homes and buildings were shattered or burned down. Among them was Jack and Goonie's house near Regents Park. They were unhurt, but Goonie, who was gravely ill with lung cancer, moved out into the countryside. Jack joined Winston and Clementine at 10 Downing Street. Winston was glad to have his brother at his side. Unlike Winston, Jack was an excellent administrator who offered to take care of much of the correspondence and financial matters for Winston. Jack also set up and ran the canteen at the Foreign Office/Downing Street complex, which allowed Winston and his team to eat wholesome meals between their endless meetings. Randolph Churchill had married just before going off to war, and his wife, Pamela, also lived with Winston and Clementine. During one of the first nights of German bombing, Pamela gave birth to a son. She named him Winston, Jr.

Like many other British families, the Churchills pitched in to help with the war effort any way they could. Sarah signed up for the Women's Auxiliary Air Force. Mary joined the Auxiliary Territorial Service and learned how to man an anti-aircraft battery. Diana served in the Women's Royal Navy Service. Randolph was a junior officer in Winston's old Queen's Hussars regiment. Clementine's main role was making sure that Winston had everything he needed to keep going. She also hosted the many people he summoned to meetings and meals. However, she wanted to be an example to other middle-aged mothers, so she volunteered to take night shifts as a firewatcher. This involved perching on rooftops during air raids watching for German incendiary bombs. These bombs were designed to start a fire a few minutes after impact. The firewatcher's job was to see where a bomb landed and race to get it raked into a sand bucket before it set anything on fire. It was tough and dangerous work, but Clementine was glad to do her part.

The bombing continued, and one evening two bombs landed at Windsor Castle, where the king and queen and their daughters Elizabeth and Margaret lived. Winston was heartened to see them appear in a news report the next day, standing resolute amid the rubble. The queen explained that many people had urged the princesses to be sent off to Canada for their safety. "The children will not leave unless I do," she said. "And I shall not leave unless their father does, and the king will not leave the country in any circumstances, whatever." This was just the message the British public needed to hear.

On September 22, 1940, two weeks after the Blitz bombing of London began, Adolf Hitler, Benito Mussolini, and Emperor Hirohito of Japan announced that they were signing a tripartite pact creating the Axis Alliance. The first two articles of the pact said it all as far as Winston was concerned:

> ARTICLE 1. Japan recognizes and respects the leadership of Germany and Italy in the establishment of a new order in Europe.

> ARTICLE 2. Germany and Italy recognize and respect the leadership of Japan in the establishment of a new order in Greater East Asia.

Japan had already invaded China in July 1937 and was running out of oil and iron ore for steelmaking, and rubber to keep their war effort going. Intelligence reports that Winston received indicated that in pursuit of these commodities, Japan was preparing to invade British, French, and Dutch colonies in Asia. Although they were a different race from the Italians and the Germans, the Japanese had embraced the same Fascist beliefs of those countries' leaders—that their civilizations were superior. They believed that they were destined by God to rule over inferior peoples and lands and that anyone who disagreed with them or stood in their way must be eliminated. Winston was glad this alliance was now out in the open. He was certain that one of those countries would make a strategic blunder. He and the British people just had to hold on until that happened.

October 15, 1940, was a particularly bad day for London. Four hundred German bombers dropped 540 tons of high explosives on the city, causing massive disruption to the entire transport network, including railways and roads. Once again Winston addressed the nation. He exhorted everyone to keep calm and carry on. Great Britain would never surrender. It would fight to the very last man.

As London was being bombed mercilessly, Winston had other important things on his mind. He pushed and pressured the United States any way he could to enter the war. He believed the Americans were Great Britain's only hope. The British couldn't hold off the Nazis singlehandedly forever. Fighting a war cost millions of pounds. Britain was quickly running out of money. Winston wrote a personal note to President Roosevelt asking for his help. Finally, it came. On March 11, 1941, President Roosevelt signed into law the Lend-Lease Act the United States Congress had passed three days before. The act authorized the president to lease or lend military hardware and supplies to any country identified as vital to the defense and security of the United States. It also opened the way for the British to receive more war supplies.

The night of May 12, 1941, after fifty-seven consecutive nights of bombing, the sky over London was eerily quiet. Winston wondered what the Germans were up to. He braced himself for what was to come. Whatever it was, it no longer seemed to include relentlessly bombing London and other British ports and industrial centers. Night after night the sky over Great Britain remained clear of bombers.

On June 22, 1941, Winston received word that Adolf Hitler had broken the German-Soviet Nonaggression Pact of 1939. This pact promised that Germany and the Soviet Union would respect each other's boundaries. Now, Germany had invaded the Soviet Union with over four million troops. It seemed foolhardy to Winston. Germany had lost the Great War in part because it fought on two fronts, the Russians in the east and the Allies in the west. Now

Adolf Hitler seemed to be repeating the same fatal error. As Winston saw it, this gave Great Britain and her Allies an opportunity to build up their weapons and resources in the west while Germany was preoccupied invading the Soviet Union.

The Soviet Union, however, could not be left to fall. If Germany and Italy successfully captured the country, the extra manpower and resources they gained would make them almost impossible to defeat. The Soviet Union had to stand strong, and now they had a common enemy in Adolf Hitler. Winston reached out to Soviet leader Joseph Stalin, offering him help in his fight against the German invasion.

A month later, Winston was off on a top-secret mission. He embarked on Great Britain's newest battleship, the *Prince of Wales,* to cross the Atlantic Ocean and rendezvoused with President Roosevelt off the coast of Newfoundland, Canada. When the two leaders got together, the president insisted he could not commit his country to go to war. The government and people of the United States would not go along with that. Instead, Roosevelt and Winston talked about other ways they could show support for each other's country. This, in turn led to the Atlantic Charter, a nonbinding treaty that affirmed that both countries stood against the aggression of the Axis powers. The charter also laid out the intention that after the war each country that was overrun by the Nazis would be liberated and allowed to govern itself.

Winston realized that this was the best outcome he could get from his meeting with President Roosevelt. He would have to continue to hold on until something happened to show the people of the United States that they could not escape the effects of war. They would not be left to live in peace indefinitely while the rest of the world was in turmoil.

Finally, the wake-up call came on Sunday, December 7, 1941. Winston had just finished dinner with two American guests when his valet brought a portable radio into the room and placed it on the mahogany side table. Winston reached over and tuned the dial to the BBC nightly news. The program was already in progress, and the three men sat listening. Suddenly there was a series of beeps. Then the BBC announcer said, "News has just been received that Japanese aircraft have raided Pearl Harbor, the American Naval Base in Hawaii. The announcement of the attack was made in a brief statement by President Roosevelt. Naval and military targets on the principal Hawaiian island of Oahu have also been attacked. No further details are yet available."

Winston jumped up and rushed to the telephone. Within minutes he was talking with President Roosevelt. "Mr. President," he said, "what's this about Japan?" Roosevelt replied, "It is true. We are all in the same boat now."

Chapter 14

"This Is Your Victory"

Winston could barely contain his relief. Great Britain no longer had to stand alone. With all the manpower and industrial strength of the United States joining the war, the Japanese attack on Pearl Harbor was the blunder he'd been waiting so long to see.

Two weeks after the attack, Winston was flying to Washington DC, with his top military aids. It was time for him and President Roosevelt to get down to business. They needed to hammer out how best to use their respective country's military and civilian strength to defeat both Nazi Germany and Japan once and for all. As dusk fell over Washington, Winston looked down at the city through the airplane window. The city was ablaze with lights, a scene he had not witnessed in two long years of war. He wiped away tears as he watched.

On Christmas Eve, President Roosevelt invited Winston to say a few words at the annual lighting of the White House Christmas tree. As he waited for his turn to speak, Winston thought about the people back home in England. Their Christmas was very different from this one here in America. There were no lighted decorations for them, no bags of candy, and no hearty meals. Food, clothing, and fuel were all heavily rationed. One in four citizens of Great Britain was in some kind of uniform. Everyone was focused on defeating the Nazis. The British people had already paid a high cost in human life. As Winston looked out over the crowd at the White House, he wondered what this gathering would look like a year from now. Would the United States be engulfed in war too, or would they help bring a swift end to the fighting? Winston couldn't have known, but he suspected they still had a long, bloody struggle ahead of them. Standing on the South Portico of the White House overlooking a crowd of fifteen thousand, Winston spoke directly to the American public:

> Let the children have their night of fun and laughter. Let the gifts of Father Christmas delight their play. Let us grown-ups share to the full in their unstinted pleasures before we turn again to the stern task and the formidable years that lie before us, resolved that, by our sacrifice and daring, these same children shall not be robbed of their inheritance or denied

their right to live in a free and decent world. And so, in God's mercy, a happy Christmas to you all.

Two days later Winston addressed a joint session of the United States Congress. Afterwards, secret talks dubbed "Operation Arcadia" began. Winston and President Roosevelt and their aides discussed the situation in the Pacific. At the same time the Japanese had attacked Pearl Harbor they attacked the British colonies of Malaya and Hong Kong and bombed Singapore. They had also attacked United States military and naval bases in Wake Island, Guam, and the Philippines. As a result, the United States was eager to fend off the Japanese, feeling they were closer to home than Germany. Winston was concerned that if the United States didn't commit to use its resources and manpower in Europe, the Germans could push on until they dominated the entire world.

After much talking and negotiating, the two leaders agreed on a "Germany First" approach. The United States would take the lead on fighting the Japanese, but they would also throw their resources behind the Allies' efforts to defeat the Germans. Once that was done, the Allies would join the United States and turn all their might on the Japanese. To do this they agreed to form a joint committee to oversee all the Allies' war efforts. Both President Roosevelt and Winston had to approve any decisions made, which in turn would stop the United States and the European Allies from duplicating their efforts. The two leaders also agreed that their first major action together would be an invasion of North Africa. In anticipation of this American bombers would be based in Great Britain. They made a pact that neither country would seek to make peace alone but would remain partners to the end.

The decisions made at the Acadia conference were unlike any that had been made before. A high level of trust would be needed between the two countries and their two leaders in combining their fighting power, armies, and navies, along with their spying and intelligence networks and weaponry technology towards one great purpose.

Winston was satisfied with the outcome of the talks. He was encouraged to see that President Franklin Roosevelt was a man of action. By the end of the week, the president promised to create a war production board with sweeping powers to control American industries. Every factory, every worker would be harnessed to turn out vast numbers of fighter planes, ships, submarines, and everything else needed to supply the Allies.

The following week, the first week of January 1942, representatives of twenty-six nations at war with the Axis powers gathered in Washington. They signed the Declaration of the United Nations and endorsed the Atlantic Charter. Together they pledged to use their full resources against the Axis and agreed never to make a separate peace.

A month after his trip to the United States, Winston awoke to grim news. Sixty thousand British troops in Singapore, once considered an island fortress, had surrendered to the Japanese. Only months before this seemed impossible, but thousands of Japanese soldiers on bicycles had peddled their way through the supposedly impenetrable jungle of the Malay peninsula and taken the British colony by surprise. Like almost everyone else, Winston found it difficult to believe.

United States military forces soon reached full capacity in the Pacific theater of war. The Americans had also cracked the Japanese message codes that told them of an impending attack on the U.S. naval base on the tiny Pacific Island of Midway. Early on the morning of June 4, airplanes from four Japanese aircraft carriers attacked and severely damaged the naval base. However, as the aircraft returned to their carriers to refuel, American planes took off from aircraft carriers hiding behind the island. The battle for control of Midway lasted two days. When it was over, the Japanese had been soundly defeated, losing around 3,000 men, four aircraft carriers, one cruiser, and hundreds of airplanes, while the United States lost approximately 362 men, one aircraft carrier, one destroyer, and nearly one hundred and fifty aircraft. Winston called President Roosevelt to congratulate him. They had proved that Japan was not invincible after all.

However, on June 20, 1942, Winston had to confront more bad news regarding British troops fighting in North Africa. Thirty-three thousand had been forced to surrender to the Germans in Tobruk, Libya. Tobruk, one of the best deep-water harbors on the Mediterranean, was now in enemy hands. Winston called the fall of Tobruk "a shattering and grievous loss."

Meanwhile, Winston continued sending secret messages to Soviet leader Joseph Stalin. Winston asked him for a face-to-face meeting so they could work together more closely. Stalin replied immediately, saying he couldn't leave Moscow as it was under threat, but he invited Winston and President Roosevelt to meet him there. Franklin Roosevelt wouldn't cross the Atlantic Ocean, but he authorized a special envoy, Averell Harriman, who was already in London, to go in his place.

Winston and Harriman flew to Moscow on August 12 for the meeting. The three participants—Winston in his one-piece zippered siren suit, Joseph Stalin in his brown communist-issue tunic, and Averell Harriman in a fashionable American suit—met at the Kremlin. Winston's first task was to give the Soviet leader the unwelcome news that they would not be opening another battlefront in Europe any time soon. Winston explained that the United States hadn't yet gotten its production of war material up to capacity and didn't think they could win a full-frontal attack on the Germans without it. Instead, Winston told Stalin that the Allies planned to invade North Africa followed by Sicily in the Mediterranean. Stalin was angry. He wanted a second front to take pressure off the Soviet forces. They were trying valiantly to prevent the Germans from capturing their oil fields in the Caucasus and from marching on Stalingrad. He accused Winston of being afraid of Hitler.

Winston stood his ground, pointing out that the United States had already sent convoys carrying weapons and military vehicles via the Arctic route to the Soviet Union. Such items could hardly be spared, but the Americans and the United Kingdom were committed to doing everything in their power to aid the Soviets.

Over three days of meetings, Stalin calmed down. He even appeared satisfied that the Allies were doing their best. Winston was also happy with the outcome. The "Big Three" needed each other to win the war. And Winston vowed that when it was over, he would manage new international relationships so the end of this war would not sow the seeds of the next. To make sure this wasn't prevented, he knew that the Soviet Union would need to be watched closely.

Finally, in November 1942, the Allies won their first major victory in the Second Battle of El Alamein in Egypt. In defeating a combined German and Italian tank and infantry force, the Allies stopped the Axis threat to Egypt, the Suez Canal, and the Middle Eastern and Persian oil fields. The victory revived Allied morale just at the right time. On the other side of North Africa, Operation Torch, under the command of U.S. Lieutenant General Dwight Eisenhower, was getting under way. A large combined Allied force came ashore at three different points on the North African coast, in Morocco, and two places in Algeria. After storming ashore, the Allied force began making its way eastward defeating or pushing back the enemy as it went.

Meanwhile, early in February 1943, after five months of fierce fighting, the battle for control of Stalingrad was over. Although nearly three-quarters of a million Soviets died defending the city, they prevailed in the end. The German army surrendered. Winston took it all as a positive sign, but he knew the war was far from over. The Japanese were closing in on New Guinea in the Pacific and Burma in Southeast Asia. And the perils of war continued out on the Atlantic Ocean, where in a four-day period in March 1943 twenty-seven merchant vessels were sunk by German U-boats.

For Winston and the Allies, more good news was at hand when on May 13, 1943, the last Axis forces in Tunisia surrendered. All North Africa was now under the control of the Allies.

Two months later the Allies invaded Sicily, and after overrunning the island, they pushed on into Italy. On September 3, Italy surrendered to the Allies. There was now one fewer enemy for the Allies to fight.

Four years had passed since Germany invaded Poland. Everyone longed for an end to the fighting, and there were glimmers of hope. The Big Three, Winston Churchill, Franklin Roosevelt, and Joseph Stalin, had all agreed to meet at the Soviet Embassy in Tehran, on November 28, 1943. Clementine and Winston's daughter Mary accompanied Winston on the trip to Iran, along with his top aides. Clementine had made her own mark in the Soviet Union as the tireless chairman of the "Aid to Russia Fund." Nearly one and a half million British workers allowed a penny a week to be deducted from their wages towards the fund. So far, the Aid to Russia Fund had raised five million pounds which had been sent to the Soviet Union to provide clothing, blankets, medical supplies, and equipment for the country's citizens. Winston was sure that his wife's dedication to raising this money for the Soviet people was helping to smooth the relationship between him and Joseph Stalin.

Although they were called the Big Three, Winston felt he'd been demoted to junior partner in the venture. He worried that he was losing his grip on the levers of international power. This was partly due to the varying sizes of the countries each leader represented. The Soviet Union had a population of 180 million people, the United States; 137 million, and the United Kingdom, 40 million. Moreover, the United States was providing most of the war material and troops in the Pacific theater to keep the war going, while Russia had vast numbers of soldiers and resources. Once Britain had stood alone, and Winston, along with his chiefs of staff, had called the shots. Now cooperation and compromise were needed.

In Tehran, even though they were allies, it was quickly apparent that each country had its own goals for the conference. Joseph Stalin kept pushing for a second battlefront to take pressure off the Soviet military. President Roosevelt insisted on a guarantee from the Soviets that once the war with Germany was over, they would continue to fight the Japanese alongside the United States. Winston was anxious to formulate plans to create a peaceful postwar Europe where human rights were respected.

By the time the Tehran conference was over, the Allies had agreed that they would invade France within six months and that the Soviet Union would fight with the Allies against Japan once the Germans were defeated.

During the conference, Winston turned sixty-nine years old. Despite this, he kept up a schedule of meetings and travel that would exhaust a man half his age. However, while traveling home to London via Tunisia, he became ill and could go no farther. The doctors who had been summoned to Carthage, Tunisia from London diagnosed Winston with pneumonia and a heart condition. For two weeks Winston lay in bed in Carthage. He missed Christmas with his family in England. It was January 12, 1944, before he was well enough to complete the journey home.

Once back in Great Britain, Winston focused on the next stage of the war—an Allied invasion of France and the final repulsing of the Nazis. If all went well, it would be the end of the German army. American General Dwight Eisenhower was put in charge of the operation, which was code-named Operation Overlord. The first phase of the plan—Operation Neptune—was to land Allied troops on the northern coast of France. It would have been much easier to invade one of the port cities, which had docks, warehouses, and roads, but they were all heavily defended by the Germans.

Winston envisioned a beach landing that would take the enemy by surprise, but it would not be easy.

The Allies would need to cross the English Channel with everything they needed—floating docks, road-making equipment, shelter, and food and weapons for over 100,000 ground troops that would go ashore on the beaches. Winston thought of the disastrous landing at Gallipoli in the Great War. Thousands of men had been slaughtered by the Turks as they came ashore. This couldn't happen again. Everything had to be meticulously planned. The soldiers must be protected at all costs.

Winston took special interest in how the men and heavy equipment would get from their ships to the beaches. He met repeatedly with army engineers to discuss ways to build artificial harbors in England that could be towed across the English Channel to France. It was an unprecedented engineering challenge. Winston insisted that these new mobile harbors include ten miles of flexible bridges that could be anchored to the sea floor and carry the weight of thirty-ton tanks, along with two miles of breakwater and floating piers that could rise and fall ten feet with the tide. They would also need to withstand the worst storms the Atlantic Ocean could throw at them. The new giant floating harbors that emerged were called Mulberries, and Winston commissioned two of them, one for the American landing site and one for the British. Forty five thousand British workers toiled away on their part of the project, building scaffolding, pouring concrete, casting anchors, and welding joints. Winston followed progress on the Mulberries and visited factories to encourage the workers.

As they prepared for Operation Overlord, the Allies took many measures to make sure the Germans didn't suspect the massive invasion. They deployed dummy armies throughout Great Britain and set up fake tanks and radio chatter to indicate that the troop buildups were to the east of the real launching points.

As the preparations neared completion, they had to decide on the day the invasion would take place. This day—D-Day—had to be perfect in so many ways. The sea had to be calm, the tide low, the moon full, and the sky cloudless for the naval vessels involved in the landing, including battleships, destroyers, minesweepers, escorts, and assault craft, to safely cross the English Channel.

Winston desperately wanted to be on hand to witness D-Day for himself. He imagined standing on the bridge of HMS *Belfast,* watching as it bombarded German positions. Of course, only Winston thought this a good idea. It was far too dangerous for the prime minister to be right in the thick of the battle. But Winston persisted. On June 4, 1944, the day before the scheduled attack, a letter arrived from King George VI informing Winston that if he insisted on being aboard a British destroyer to observe the invasion, then he, the king, would be coming along as well. Reading this, Winston quickly backed down. There was no way he could allow the king to risk his life.

Before the planned invasion, Winston told Dwight Eisenhower, "I am in this thing with you to the end, and if it fails, we will go down together."

The weather on June 4 was calm, but the top military meteorologist predicted that a huge storm was coming. The invasion was postponed an agonizing twenty-four hours. The following day wind and rain lashed southern England as predicted, but the meteorologist pointed out a pocket of calm weather for the next day. With this information, General Eisenhower gave the order that Operation Overlord would begin on June 6.

The D-Day invasion was a massive operation, unlike anything the world had ever experienced. While submarines lay submerged off the north coast of France, gliders silently dropped paratroopers along the coast. Naval ships then descended upon the scene escorted by minesweepers. All in all, seven thousand boats and ships ferried supplies and men across the English Channel. They also protected the 132,000 troops from fifteen Allied nations as they waded through the waves and onto the beaches of northern France. As the soldiers came ashore, four thousand bombers and thirty-seven hundred fighter aircraft provided air support, pounding German coastal defenses with bombs and machine gun fire.

Winston sat in the Cabinet War Rooms complex in London listening to every message. Few German U-boats were spotted, and the Luftwaffe remained, for the most part, on the ground, a sure sign that they had been caught by surprise. It all boded well for the Allies. As causality reports rolled in, Winston learned that four thousand Allied soldiers had been killed during the first day. He breathed a sigh of relief. The casualty count had been predicted to be much higher, perhaps as many as twenty thousand dead. The beaches had been secured, and one hundred tugboats had towed the two Mulberries piece by piece across the English Channel to their resting places. Once assembled, each Mulberry could handle ten thousand tons of supplies per day, enough to keep twenty-five divisions supplied.

The Allies pushed on after their landing but at a slower pace than predicted. It was five more days before men and equipment from the five separate landing beaches were able to join forces. Together they formed a front sixty miles long and fifteen miles deep. They were ready to push the Germans out of France all the way back to their homeland.

On June 12, it was deemed safe enough for Winston to visit the newly liberated beaches of Normandy, France. He sailed across the English Channel aboard HMS *Kelvin* to see the Mulberries in action. He was impressed with how effective they had been.

The following day, plane spotters along the southern coast of England reported a strange sight. They described it as resembling a small airplane with short wings and a fire in its tail, flying towards London at about 350 miles per hour. It was, as Winston feared, the first of thousands of V-1 flying bombs, a new type of weapon the Germans were launching from sites in France. Within days, up to one hundred V-1 bombs were falling every hour over South London. Each of these bombs had an 1,870-pound warhead capable of destroying an entire street or factory. Some were shot down or intercepted by aircraft, but many of the bombs found their targets, killing hundreds of people a day. Winston knew that the only solution to the problem was for the Allies to push the Germans out of France and Belgium, which would deprive them of their launching sites. Until then, the British people would have to be resolute.

On July 16, 1944, the French port of Cherbourg was cleared of mines, finally giving the Allies a sheltered harbor to land their supplies. The Allies then began making steady progress, forcing the German army to retreat. On August 23, the Allies liberated Paris. Winston was in Italy at the time and feeling sick. Two days later he was diagnosed with pneumonia again and put on an airplane back to England. His temperature had soared to 103 degrees Fahrenheit by the time Clementine met him. Winston's doctor prescribed him a new miracle drug called penicillin. The drug worked, and Winston made a complete recovery.

The Big Three Allied leaders met again on February 4, 1945, at Yalta, on the Black Sea coast of Crimea. They congratulated each other on the success of Operation Overlord. Everyone was confident that it was only a matter of time before the Nazis buckled and surrendered. The agenda for the meeting at Yalta was to make final plans for entering Germany and determine what to do after its surrender. Should Poland be free or annexed by the Soviet Union? And how would they establish a new alliance of peaceful countries, dubbed the United Nations?

It should have been the meeting of three equals who had fought side by side, but it wasn't. Each of the Allies had its own reasons for uniting, and now those reasons were beginning to tear them apart. Winston noticed how ill President Roosevelt looked. He seemed to be having difficulty concentrating for long periods and drifted off from the conversation. But through it all, Stalin stayed laser focused.

Winston was astounded at the lack of interest Roosevelt paid to the issues at hand. The president told Stalin that the United States intended to stay in Europe for only two years once the war ended. Winston watched Stalin's eyes light up at this. He knew it would take much longer to stabilize Germany and didn't like the idea of having to negotiate alone with Joseph Stalin after the Americans left. Some agreements were made during the meetings, but mostly the three leaders could agree only to give matters "further consideration." Winston returned to London with a sense of dread. The war would not truly be over in a month or a year, even a decade. Long after the guns fell silent, millions of men, women, and children would have to live with the consequences of decisions made at conferences like Yalta.

Six weeks after the meeting in Yalta, the Allies crossed the Rhine River and entered Germany on March 22–24, 1945. The move was accompanied by massive bombing of German industrial cities, including Dresden and Berlin.

Winston was informed that President Franklin Roosevelt had died on April 12, 1945, and that Vice President Harry Truman was about to be sworn in as the next president of the United States. Two weeks later, Winston learned that Italian dictator Benito Mussolini had been captured while fleeing to Switzerland and was executed by firing squad. Then on April 30, Adolf Hitler committed suicide in a bunker in Berlin. Winston was glad to hear the news. He'd been concerned that even in defeat, Hitler would still have the power to influence others to take up his Fascist cause.

On May 8, 1945, Winston received the news he'd been waiting so long to hear: Germany had unconditionally surrendered to the Allies. Huge crowds gathered in every public square across the United Kingdom, bands played, and people danced and sang. Winston drove through the streets of London in an open car, waving the victory sign as the crowds cheered. He then addressed the people from the balcony at Whitehall. Five years had passed since he had taken over leadership of the country and its war effort. At that time, he had promised the people of Great Britain victory at any cost. Now that day had arrived. "This is your victory," he told the crowd. "Everyone, man or woman, has done their best.... God bless you all!"

"No, this is your victory," the crowd yelled back. And indeed, in many ways it was. Winston Churchill had never wavered, never doubted, never flagged during the ordeal of war he and his countrymen had endured. By sheer resolute willpower, he had pulled the nation through the unimaginable to victory.

Chapter 15

Sir Winston Churchill

After the war in Europe ended, fighting continued to rage on in the Pacific theater. The Japanese appeared determined to fight to the last man, despite it being impossible for them to win now with the full might of the Allies focused on them.

In Great Britain, not every soldier who fought in Europe could come home immediately. Many tasks still needed to be taken care of. In particular, Germany needed to be stabilized. About twenty-two million people lived in the British occupational zone in northwestern Germany, a great many of them homeless and helpless, orphans and widows, or maimed and lost. Railroads, streets, and factories across the area were smashed, as were schools and hospitals. When the British took on the role of occupiers, they became responsible for feeding them all, restoring industry, transportation links, and other infrastructure, as well as conducting trials to hold Nazi leaders accountable. It was important that justice was seen to be served, especially on those who oversaw the concentration camps where approximately six million European Jews, five million Soviet prisoners of war, and other victims had been exterminated.

Things in Great Britain did not go back to normal right away either. Virtually every family in the country had been affected through the bombings or other aspects of the fighting. In some cities, particularly London, whole neighborhoods were destroyed, and adequate housing was now in short supply. Rationing also became stricter as food and fuel supplies now had to be shared with those living in the British-occupied sector of Germany.

In Great Britain, everyone was asking the same question: What did the future hold for them, the country, and the British Empire? In the lead up to war, as well as during it, the normal general election cycle had been interrupted. A general election hadn't been held for ten years. For the last five years of the war, Winston's government was a coalition one. But with the war in Europe over, it was time for another election.

The Conservative Party was confident it would win the election based on how Winston had led the country to victory. Polls showed his personal popularity steady at around eighty percent. But other factors were in play. The men and women of Great Britain, both those who stayed home and those who went to fight, wanted better opportunities and a more equal society now that the war was over. In 1942 a three-hundred-page report from economist Sir William Beverage proposed a sweeping plan to change many aspects of British society. The report suggested that many of Great Britain's largest industries, such as coal mining, electricity generation and distribution, and the railways, be brought under state control. It also called for the establishment of various social services, such as a National Health Service to provide free health care to everyone, better housing, and unemployment benefits, disability benefits, and old-age pensions. The report painted a future where the taxes British citizens paid would guarantee them all a basic standard of living from cradle to grave. As the election approached, the Labour Party promised that if elected, it would implement the Beverage Report recommendations.

The election was held on Thursday, July 5, 1945, and the result was stark. The Labour Party swept to victory. Churchill was out, and Clement Attlee was Great Britain's new prime minister. Like many others, Winston was shocked and disappointed by the result, but he refused to complain. He had lost in a fair election, and fair elections were at the heart of democracy—the very thing the country had gone to war to protect.

On Thursday evening, July 26, Winston was driven to Buckingham Palace to hand in his resignation as prime minister to King George VI. He remembered back five years before when the king had summoned him and asked him to form a war government. What a journey those five years had been for him, for Great Britain, and for the whole world. The Allies had prevailed in Europe, and Winston was confident that they would soon do so in the Pacific.

Winston's confidence in the outcome of the war in the Pacific and Southeast Asia was partly due to something top secret. It was so top secret that President Roosevelt hadn't even told his vice president. Harry Truman learned of it only after President Roosevelt died and he became president. This secret was the Manhattan Project. During the war the United States, Great Britain, and Canada had been working together to build the world's first atomic bomb. This weapon was designed to create a nuclear fission reaction that would unleash a massive amount of energy from atoms in a catastrophic chain reaction. Ten days before the results of the election were announced, Winston learned that President Truman intended to use an atomic bomb against Japan if the country refused to surrender.

For the three months after the end of the war in Europe, the Japanese fought on in the Pacific. As they became more desperate, they introduced new tactics. One of the scariest was kamikaze attacks. In these attacks a lone pilot would crash a fuel-heavy, bomb-laden aircraft into an Allied ship. It was a suicide mission that changed the protocols of war. The human toll was enormous. Close to five thousand U.S. sailors were killed in these kamikaze attacks, and five thousand more were wounded. In a short period of time, the Allies lost thirty ships, and around four hundred others were damaged.

Despite the suicide attacks, the Allies were inching their way, battle by battle, towards the Japanese archipelago. Winston watched and waited, hoping that the Japanese would accept that they would lose and then surrender. He knew that American military commanders had calculated that between half a million and a million Allied soldiers could be killed if they had to invade Japan. But even as the Japanese casualty count soared in the fighting, their leaders refused to admit defeat. And so, the final decision was made. On August 6, 1945, an America Boeing B-29 Superfortress bomber dropped an atomic bomb on the Japanese city of Hiroshima. The bomb leveled five square miles of the city, instantly obliterating about eighty thousand men, women, and children.

The Japanese still refused to surrender. A second atomic bomb was dropped on the city of Nagasaki on August 9, again with devastating results. This time Japan truly understood that the Allies could not be stopped. On August 15, Japan's emperor announced the country's surrender at the Allies. The Second World War was officially over on all fronts.

Although no longer prime minister, Winston was still an elected member of the House of Commons. He did all he could in Parliament to influence foreign policies. It worried him greatly that of the Big Three Allied leaders, Joseph Stalin was the only one still in power. It felt to Winston as though he, Franklin Roosevelt, and Joseph Stalin had all been playing a giant chess game. Now Stalin had the board all to himself, and he would take full advantage of that situation. And he did. Stalin swept aside the Atlantic

Charter that Winston and President Roosevelt had agreed to in August 1941. This had promised that every country liberated during the war would be free to determine its own future. That goal seemed far away now. Soviet troops had ensconced themselves in the Eastern European countries they liberated and showed no signs of leaving.

This also presented a problem for the newly formed United Nations. The Soviet Union was a founding member and along with China, France, the United Kingdom, and the United States, was a permanent member of the United Nations Security Council. Each permanent member country could veto any resolutions put forward by other members of the council. It became increasingly difficult to hold meaningful debate, with the Soviets always threatening to veto motions put forward by other council members, particularly the United States and the United Kingdom. As a result, Winston dedicated much of his time and energy towards making the United Nations work. He believed the organization was key to preventing another catastrophic war somewhere in the world.

Seven months after the war ended, in March 1946, Winston and Clementine flew to Cuba. Fifty-one years had passed since twenty-year-old Winston first arrived in the island nation. Then he'd been in search of an adventurous war. Now he was committed to doing everything in his power to create a world at peace.

From Cuba the Churchills flew to Washington DC, from where they accompanied President Truman on his presidential train to his home state of Missouri. They visited Westminster College in Fulton, Missouri, where Winston was conferred with an honorary degree. As part of the ceremony, Winston had been asked to make a speech. It was supposed to be an encouraging speech about how the world was a better place now that Nazi Germany had been defeated, but Winston had other thoughts on his mind.

Standing before the crowd of students gathered in the college's gymnasium, Winston told them that the Allies had fought hard to get to a place of peace, but now the Soviet Union was the biggest threat to that peace. He explained that Stalin respected strength and that Great Britain and the United States would lose any negotiation with him unless they showed they were willing to back it up with action. So far, the Soviet Union's actions proved they weren't interested in democracy, no matter what they might say. In fact, Stalin was in the process of annexing the countries the Soviets had liberated from the Germans in Eastern Europe and turning them into Soviet Socialist Republics. In those annexed countries and territories dissenting voices had fallen ominously silent. Communism was trying to swallow up democracy. Or as Winston put it, "An iron curtain has descended across the continent."

The reaction to Winston's speech at Westminster College was swift. Even Eleanor Roosevelt, President Roosevelt's widow, declared her outrage over what Winston had said. Now, she and many others argued, was not the time to split the Allies. The United Kingdom, the United States, and the Soviet

Union needed to walk arm in arm into the future, even if they did have different styles of government.

Winston didn't really care about the thoughts and reactions of people to his speech. He had foreseen the Nazi uprising in Germany and warned about it, but no one took notice until it was too late. Now he was convinced that the Soviet Union would betray the alliances it had made with democratic countries as soon as it was expedient for them to do so. He felt compelled to warn people about it.

Upon returning to Great Britain, Winston began work on his next ambitious project—a six-volume series of books analyzing World War II. Winston hired a team of research assistants, military experts, secretaries, and ghostwriters to work with him. As he left office as prime minister, Winston struck a unique bargain with the cabinet secretary, Sir Edward Bridges. Winston asked that many official wartime papers be classified as his personal property. Sir Edward agreed, on the condition that before the books went to print the government got to approve the final draft of any books that quoted the papers. Since it would be fifty years before the documents were declassified for the public, Winston had a tremendous advantage over anyone trying to compile an account of the war, at least from the British perspective.

During this time, Winston took several long holidays, mainly to the south of France. He always took a writing project and his easel and paints along with him. Sometimes he traveled alone, sometimes with Clementine and their daughter Diana.

On Tuesday, February 11, 1947, Winston walked his youngest daughter Mary down the aisle as she married Christopher Soames. He was a war hero who was awarded the French Croix de Guerre for his actions at the Second Battle of El Alamein in 1942. Unlike Winston and Clementine's other children, Mary quickly settled into a drama-free marriage. She and Christopher moved onto the farm at Chartwell.

By now oldest daughter Diana had divorced and was remarried to her second husband, conservative politician Duncan Sandy. The couple had three children, Julian, Edwina, and Celia. Son Randolph and his wife, Pamela, were separated and working on a divorce.

Mary and Christopher's wedding was quickly followed by a funeral. Twelve days after their marriage, Winston's sixty-seven-year-old brother Jack died. He had been ill for a long time, but Winston was still devastated by his death. The two brothers had stuck together through thick and thin, on the battlefield during the Boer War, and in the trenches on the Western Front in France during the Great War. Jack had also done a lot of research for and advised Winston on his books and managed the family's money through good times and bad. Now it was all over. The weather was particularly cold at the time of Jack's death, and as much as Winston wanted to attend his funeral in Bladon, his doctor forbade him from traveling there. His own health was deteriorating, and for once he obeyed his doctor.

Things seemed to be falling apart around Winston. Although he argued forcefully in Parliament, he couldn't stop great swathes of the British Empire separating from "Mother England." Following the passing of the Indian Independence Act in July 1947, two independent nations, India and Pakistan, were created from the old British India. Following the founding of the East India Company in 1600, British merchants and Great Britain itself had dominated and controlled the subcontinent of India for nearly 350 years. Now, despite Winston's strenuous objection, the Labour government had given India independence. The British Empire, which Winston had pledged his life to protect, was fast transforming into a voluntary network of independent and equal countries now called the British Commonwealth.

On February 23, 1950, a general election was held in Great Britain. Clement Attlee and the Labour Party won by just five seats. Twenty months later, Clement Attlee called a snap election, hoping to increase his party's majority in the House of Commons. It was held on October 9, 1951. The move backfired. Labour was voted out. The Conservative Party won the election, and Winston was still party leader. This meant that at seventy-nine years of age, Winston Churchill was once again prime minister of Great Britain. Winston hadn't expected this in his old age but embraced the challenge. He set two ambitious goals for this term as prime minister: First, to strengthen the special bond that existed between the United States and Great Britain. He saw this bond as vital to protecting world peace. Second, to expand communication with the Soviet Union, also in the pursuit of peace and to stave off another war in Europe.

Winston and Clementine moved back into 10 Downing Street, the prime minister's official residence. They had barely settled in when news came that King George VI had died at the age of fifty-six. His twenty-five-year-old daughter was on her way back to London from Kenya, where she had been on a state visit. She was now Great Britain's new monarch, Queen Elizabeth II.

Winston was fond of the new queen. He remembered her courage as a teenager during the war, how she kept living in the palace after it was bombed. She had also trained as an ambulance mechanic and tended her own "Dig for Victory" garden at Windsor Castle.

As he had done with her father, Winston continued the tradition of meeting with young Queen Elizabeth every Tuesday evening. He used this time to brief her as to what was happening in government. He discovered that the new queen had a wonderful sense of humor and that she appreciated the time he spent advising her and answering questions.

Winston's niece Clarissa, Jack and Goonie's daughter, was married August 14, 1952, in London to conservative politician Anthony Eden. Winston and Clementine stood in for her parents and also held a reception for the newlyweds at 10 Downing Street.

In spring 1953, a year after her ascension to the throne of Great Britain, Queen Elizabeth II knighted Winston for his lifetime of service to the country. He was now Sir Winston Churchill, and Clementine was Lady Churchill.

That summer Winston suffered a stroke that paralyzed him on his left side. Sadly, his successor, Anthony Eden, Clarissa's husband, was in no condition to take over as prime minister. He had recently had his appendix removed, but the surgery was botched, and he required several more operations to save his life. As a result, Winston's stroke was kept a secret from the British public. With grit and determination, Winston clawed his way back to health. Three months after his stroke, Winston was back in Parliament giving a speech. His doctor, Lord Moran, couldn't believe it and told Winston afterwards that he was an astonishing creature who did not follow the rules of nature.

In October 1953, Sir Winston Churchill learned that he was to be awarded the Nobel Prize in Literature in December "for his mastery of historical and biographical description as well as for brilliant oratory in defending exalted human values." The award was a great honor, and no one could deny that it was well deserved. As December approached, Winston learned that he needed to travel to Bermuda to attend a rescheduled conference with President Dwight Eisenhower. In his stead, Clementine and Mary traveled to Sweden to accept Winston's Nobel Prize.

By April 1955, even Winston had to admit it was time to resign as prime minister. His farewell was an epic affair. Queen Elizabeth II and her husband, Prince Philip, even accepted an invitation to dine at 10 Downing Street with thirty of Winston's closest friends and colleagues. The next night, at his usual and last Tuesday night meeting with the queen, he handed in his resignation as prime minister of the United Kingdom.

Anthony Eden took over as prime minister, but true to form, Winston retained his seat as a member of the House of Commons. Even at eighty years of age, he still had a voice and was determined to use it to the end.

Chapter 16

In Grateful Remembrance

After retiring from being prime minister, Winston turned his energy to completing a writing project he had begun years before. The four-volume series of books under the title *A History of the English-Speaking Peoples* covered the period between the Roman invasions of Britain and the end of the Second Boer War.

Now that he was eighty years old, Winston slackened his workload a little. He took longer holidays in the south of France and enjoyed long cruises with his friend Aristotle Onassis aboard his yacht in the Mediterranean. Winston and Clementine also made regular visits to the United States. Despite his more relaxed pace, Winston managed to finish all four volumes of *A History of the English-Speaking Peoples*. The volumes were published between 1956 and 1958.

As the years went by, Winston suffered a series of ministrokes. Although he worked hard to bounce back from them, his stamina was slowly ebbing.

On April 9, 1963, President John F. Kennedy declared Winston Churchill an honorary citizen of the United States by Act of Congress. Winston was the first person to be given such an honor. Sadly, he was too weak to attend the ceremony in person, and his son Randolph and grandson Winston Jr. traveled to accept the honor on his behalf. Winston also spent most of his time at the house that he and Clementine kept at 28 Hyde Park Gate in central London, as it was located closer to doctors and hospitals.

In October 1963, his daughter Diana died unexpectedly. She was fifty-four years old. When Winston heard the news, he barely spoke. He sat and stared out the window for hours, tears sliding down his cheeks. Old age had both its triumphant moments and its bitter ones.

Although becoming increasingly deaf and forgetful, Winston stubbornly refused to give up his seat in the House of Commons. As long as he was able to vote, he wanted to stay engaged in politics. However, at age eighty-nine, even he had to admit his time in public life had run its course. Winston Churchill's name did not appear on any ballot in the 1964 general election, for the first time in sixty-four years. His amazing achievements were honored by Parliament. He had served in the United Kingdom's Parliament for two-thirds of a century, under thirteen prime ministers. He also served two terms as prime minister. And he had lived during the reigns of six British monarchs, four kings and two queens.

On the eve of his ninetieth birthday, around a thousand people gathered in the rain outside Winston's London house to sing him "Happy Birthday." As he stood at the window, old memories flooded back. He thought of the time he received a hero's welcome in Durban following his escape from the Boer prisoner of war camp and of the crowd gathered outside Whitehall cheering him when news came of Germany's surrender. He had been privileged to be a part of such a swath of world history.

On January 15, 1965, Winston Churchill suffered a major stroke and slipped into a coma. Queen Elizabeth II and the prime minister were informed. The United Kingdom braced itself.

A blizzard had been howling on the morning of January 24, 1895, when Winston rushed across Hyde Park to be with his dying father. Now, on January 24, 1965, exactly seventy years later to the day, Winston himself lay dying. Clementine, who'd shared his trials and triumphs for fifty-six years, sat holding his hand. His remaining children, Randolph, Sarah, and Mary, along with several grandchildren stood quietly at the foot of the bed as Winston Churchill took his last breath.

Queen Elizabeth II gifted Winston Churchill a State Funeral, something normally reserved for the reigning monarch. In truth, the funeral plans had been years in the making, with Winston helping to plan it himself. "Operation Hope Not," as it was called, was his last logistical triumph.

Every honor was afforded Winston. His coffin lay in state in the Palace of Westminster for three days. The hall was open twenty-three hours a day, and a continual line of people, often over a mile long, waited to view his coffin and pay their last respects to Winston.

Sir Winston Churchill's funeral was held at St. Paul's Cathedral, with Queen Elizabeth II and Prince Phillip breaking protocol to attend the service. Kings, queens, presidents, and prime ministers came from around the world. All in all, 120 nations were represented. An estimated 350 million people from as far afield as Pakistan and New Zealand watched the service on black-and-white television sets. This made it the biggest televised event in history.

After the funeral service, Winston's coffin was carried from St. Paul's to the Tower of London by Grenadier Guards. There it was loaded onto a government launch. The man who had been First Lord of the Admiralty twice made one last voyage: up the river Thames to Waterloo Station. As the launch passed Hays Wharf, thirty-six dock workers lowered their crane jibs one after the other in a spontaneous salute while sixteen fighter jets from the Royal Air Force dipped their wings overhead.

At Waterloo Station the coffin was loaded onto a specially built train car, which was hitched to the "Winston Churchill" engine, a steam locomotive that had been named in honor of Winston in 1947. As the train puffed slowly through the Oxfordshire countryside, thousands of people lined the tracks to pay homage to the man who had inspired them in their hour of crisis. Many wore their old military uniforms and saluted as the coffin passed.

Sir Winston Churchill was buried in the graveyard of St. Martin's Church, Bladon, near his birthplace at Blenheim Palace. Beside him were his mother, father, and brother Jack. On the day of his burial, two wreaths were placed at the head of his grave. The first, from Queen Elizabeth II, had a note attached that read, "From the nation and the Commonwealth in grateful remembrance, Elizabeth R." The second wreath was from Clementine. Her note read, "I will soon be with you again."

Bibliography

Churchill, Randolph S. *Winston S. Churchill: Young Statesman 1901–1914*. Houghton Mifflin, 1967.

Churchill, Winston. *My Early Life: 1874–1904*. Scribner, 1930.

D'Este, Carlo. *Warlord: A Life of Winston Churchill at War, 1874–1945*. Harper, 2008.

Lee, Celia and John. *The Churchills: A Family Portrait*. Palgrave Macmillan, 2010.

Lee, Celia and John. *Winston and Jack: The Churchill Brothers*. Celia Lee, 2007.

Manchester, William and Paul Reid. & Reid, Paul, *The Last Lion: Winston Churchill Defender of the Realm, 1940–1965*. Bantam Books, 2012.

Purnell, Sonia. *Clementine: The Life of Mrs. Winston Churchill*. Viking, 2015.

Read, Simon. *Winston Churchill Reporting: Adventures of a Young War Correspondent.* Da Capo Press, 2015.

Roberts, Andrew. *Churchill: Walking with Destiny.* Viking, 2018.

About the Authors

Janet and Geoff Benge are a husband and wife writing team with more than thirty years of writing experience. Janet is a former elementary school teacher. Geoff holds a degree in history. Originally from New Zealand, the Benges spent ten years serving with Youth With A Mission. They have two daughters, Laura and Shannon, and an adopted son, Lito. They make their home in the Orlando, Florida, area.

Heroes of History are available in paperback, e-book, and audiobook formats, with more coming soon! Unit Study Curriculum Guides are available for each biography.

www.heroesofhistory.com